I already know this is a book that I will re[ad] guide. It provides both a framework an[d] reader to discover who they really are an[d] must find that out and put it into action.

Jane Gunn – The Barefoot Mediator and author, *The Mole and the Mountain*

Absolutely loved this book. The combination of autobiography, biography and insightful personal development makes it a recipe for success. Captivating, educational and entertaining, this book is a trifecta of great reading. Its unique format will spur your personal growth no matter what your age. The author's viewpoints, combined with her grandfather's prisoner of war experiences, create a superb and compelling read. I read it in one sitting and then went back to study it again.

Tim Durkin – healthcare leadership expert

In an age where storytelling is a vital skill, *Focus on Why* shines as a beautiful example of this art, steeped in wisdom and insight.

Amy masterfully weaves her purpose framework into her narrative, making the lessons and questions land deeply and resonate with the reader. There is a delightful cleverness in how she integrates these elements organically, avoiding any sense of clunkiness or predictability.

This charming tale of her own personal family history will stay with you long after you've turned the last page. It's a book that doesn't just tell a story but also has the power to change lives, offering profound reflections and practical guidance. *Focus on Why* is more than just a read; it's an experience that promises to transform your perspective and ignite your purpose.

Helen Chorley – angel investor, board advisor and keynote speaker

Wow! Just wow! Have you ever read a book that gives you goosebumps and makes you cry – more than once? This book has done this and so much more. I love how Amy Rowlinson has intertwined her life, her grandfather's life and her podcast with her nine-step framework to truly help me focus on my life's purpose, to stop talking about it and take action on it.

Having read this book, I realise I've been stuck in the 'plan' stage because I never knew the impact of going through the 'purpose' stage or the value of the 'focus' stage. Every day I am closer to my death day and this book has made me realise that I have been talking about my life purpose for the last ten years. And whilst I have had coaches and made plans, I have always let life's circumstances get in the way and stop me. By knowing the controllables, I am now going to stop these life circumstances taking control of my life and instead plan my life of purpose with Mark, my husband. He has also had big plans, but never had the big vision of how to get there. Using this book and its framework, together we will do this.

Vicky O'Farrell – people expert and CEO and founder, Queen of Behaviours

This is a beautiful gift, a golden opportunity for you to look at your current reality in relation to your values and purpose. If these are not aligned then Amy provides suggestions and solutions to change that so you can feel connected to your purpose and therefore to yourself. The book takes you on a journey through Amy and George's stories of purpose, both of which are extraordinary and moving. I can't recommend this book highly enough. It will be with you for life.

Charlotte Jones – nutritionist, physiotherapist, author and lecturer

In what is the most unique book I've ever had the privilege of reading, George's wisdom is both simple and powerful, making it truly effective. Amy has continued to use this wisdom to grow, evolve and develop a passionate curiosity, dedicating herself to creating a planned and meaningful life.

Amy's profound insights and actionable advice offer a refreshing perspective that purpose isn't something we find externally but something we create and feel from within.

This book isn't just about finding your why; it's about crafting a life filled with meaning and intentionality, aligning actions with values for genuine fulfilment.

Focus on Why is a compelling and warm invitation to step out of the fog of mere existence and into a life of vibrant purpose. Amy's own journey, shared with raw honesty and rich storytelling, creates a personal connection that resonates deeply, making this book not just a read, but an experience of transformation.

If you're ready to stop searching and start living with intention, *Focus on Why* is the roadmap you've been waiting for. I feel beyond privileged to have had the opportunity to learn from these lessons and this intensely lived experience.

It is a breathtakingly powerful read and I truly appreciate the gift Amy has given me.

Kim-Adele Randall – CEO, Authentic Achievements

Sinek said start with it, Rowlinson says focus on it! This great book helps you challenge the status quo, define your purpose and focus on your why – all three things that are currently lacking in society today. Told through the brilliant story of George F Kerr, rekindled from his scrapbook, *Focus on Why* is not only a befitting tribute but a brilliantly simple framework to map your own journey through life. Stop existing, start living, and 'tap into the tingle'. Get *Focus on Why*!

Wing Commander Marcus Dimbleby, RAF (retd) – MD and founder, Effective Direction™

keep challenging the status quo.

Much love

Amy x

FOCUS ON
WHY

Create a purposeful way of life

Amy Rowlinson
with George Fleming Kerr

Focus on Why
ISBN 978-1-915483-29-4 (paperback)
ISBN 978-1-915483-30-0 (ebook)

Published in 2024 by Right Book Press
Printed in the UK

A CIP record of this book is available from the British Library.

My gratitude goes to those who've shaped my life:
My grandfather's stepmother, Amie – gentle guidance
My grandparents, Ruth and George – unconditional love and curiosity
My parents, Catharine and Tony – creativity, adventure and independence
My husband, Jon – unwavering support, love and patience
My children, Holly and Eddie – inspiration, joy and possibility

25 March 1945

This record has dragged its weary course across Europe and the Greater German Reich, through the gates of the prison and into the cell itself, to the bunk in a corner there – the very centre and soul of prison life. Any account of this life will be interesting for as much as it treats not of the prison but the mind and the spirit held there.

Contents

Foreword

L ast December I looked at my small grandchildren and wondered what the world would be like when they are my age. I became very upset and began asking myself, 'What does the world need and what can I do about it?'

The answer I came up with is that the world needs genius ideas. I'm a neuroscientist and a good communicator but I'm not a genius. Then it struck me… and my purpose was born.

I'm meant to work with geniuses and the most unsuspecting people to help tease out their genius ideas and communicate them to gain support, funding and investment in the STEM industries. This is how I can help the next generation.

I've known Amy Rowlinson for some time now through work and friendship, and it's her relentless belief in purpose that sowed the seed for me to make more of my own life and use my skills and talents for the greater good, and it feels incredible. Work doesn't feel like work. That's the point – feelings. Amy taught me that purpose feels as though you have 'come home', that all the jigsaw pieces fit together, and if you read this book, you'll understand what I mean.

Focus on Why is full of extracts from a man's WW2 prisoner of war journals and letters interwoven with Amy's life today, both of which focus on purpose. The fact that this man is Amy's grandfather makes for a glorious adventure for the reader whilst all the time learning about her nine-step framework to help you to create a life of purpose and fulfilment.

Imagine what it must feel like to write a book with your deceased grandfather. This has blown me away. It's rare that I'm completely captivated by a book. This means that *Focus on Why* is a rare book indeed. It is enlightening, sensitive and historical and it reaches the soul. The reader is enveloped in two worlds separated by time but entwined by love and common purpose.

Amy also has an extremely successful podcast called *Focus on WHY* that has been going strong since 2020. She has a talent for getting the most out of her guests in a way that is encouraging and sometimes even unexpected. If you haven't encountered it yet, seek it out and see what you think. It's helpful to listen to other people speak about purpose.

So are you ready to dive into this well-researched and unique book? To read something that's so worthwhile? To feel better about yourself and perhaps find something to focus on that has greater meaning? To help alleviate some of the anxieties of uncertainty and much more? Then this is a book of insights and learnings whilst also being a thing of beauty which will have you transfixed.

I honestly believe Amy's work is going to help more people than she can ever imagine.

Thank you, Amy.

Dr Lynda Shaw, behavioural neuroscientist, genius mentor and author, *Your Brain Is Boss* **and** *Beat the Bullies: Use Your Brain*

Introduction

Challenge the Status Quo

Does your life lack purpose and direction? Are you feeling unfulfilled in life and work? Do you long to make a difference but feel overwhelmed by daily demands? In striving for that 'perfect' life, are you sacrificing your health to the point of burnout? Or are you sleep-walking, drifting aimlessly and mindlessly scrolling on social media or binge-watching TV?

Rest assured that if any of these resonate with you, you're not alone. In today's fast-paced, materialistic world, there's huge pressure to seek instant gratification, accumulate bigger, better, shinier possessions and strike that perfect work–life balance.

So if you're stressed, frustrated, confused or facing uncertainty, it's time to challenge the status quo, spark a re-evaluation of your past and future, and take personal responsibility to live authentically. It's for you to choose what happens next. Welcome to the purpose party!

Focus on Why

For some, searching for purpose is an overcomplicated, elusive, seemingly impossible pursuit, and as a coach I witness the anxiety people experience when they haven't been able to find or define their purpose. Unable to answer the questions 'Who am I, what is my purpose, and what am I supposed to be doing with my life?', panic sets in, building into an existential crisis. When they see clarity of purpose in others, I often hear them ask, frustrated, 'Well, how do I find my why?'

If you're trying to find your why, please stop searching! The truth is

1

you don't find your why by looking for it **externally**; you **create** and **feel** it from **within** and this is often where the confusion lies. Your **why** and **purpose** are not the same, but they are interconnected.

Purpose is the overarching intention that guides your direction in life, and it's whatever you choose it to be. It's as simple as that.

Your **why** is the emotional significance you assign to your purpose.

Serving as your biggest intrinsic motivator, your why provides you with the commitment and focus needed to achieve all intentions aligned with your purpose.

The why emerges from **reflection**, while purpose is created through subsequent **action**. Through the process of reflection, you gain clarity and valuable insights into your inner world, interpreting and uncovering the meaning of your experiences and understanding your next steps. Reflection helps you identify patterns, overcome limiting beliefs or behaviours, and explore biases, strengths and areas for growth, all while helping align your actions with your values and aspirations.

Continually reflect on your actions and adjust your course as needed to develop resilience and adaptability in the face of challenges. Intentional action is vital for achieving goals and living a fulfilling life. Your future success is therefore dependent on the actions you take after reflecting, as without action, your dreams will remain dreams.

Without a defined understanding of meaning and purpose, you might find yourself merely reacting to events rather than recognising how they each hold a meaningful significance that contributes to guiding your intentional actions and achieving fulfilment. When you couple reflection with action, that's when true growth occurs. This incredible transformation is achieved through the exploratory method I call Reflection with Action.

Fuelled by deep, purposeful reflection, your actions become a catalyst for positive change, igniting powerful ripple effects that extend far beyond your immediate influence to create lasting impact. Focus on developing your internal understanding of how to respond effectively through the practice of Reflection with Action rather than searching for an external why.

Living with purpose isn't a singular goal to achieve; instead it enables you to derive value and meaning from multiple sources as you transition through each stage of life. Purpose requires ongoing reassessment. What once provided fulfilment or significance at age 20 may not still resonate when you're 30, 50 or 70. Acknowledging this shift enables you to plan and adapt your own flourishing lifestyle as your purpose evolves. Embracing this responsibility to continuously focus on your why and understand what holds meaning for you initiates a lifelong exploration of self-discovery and growth involving three elements: a purpose, a plan and a focus on why. Accordingly, this book is divided into three parts, which together form the necessary framework to create a purposeful way of life.

Acceptance of your mortality is key to understanding your life's purpose. Pausing to think about your identity, actions and motivations can reveal the truth about your current self and your future trajectory. As you face many choices and decisions, view them as opportunities for new beginnings, knowing that you can always change direction and make decisions that shape your future. Focusing on your why defines your lifestyle, driven by what inspires, motivates and guides you.

Regardless of circumstances, you are responsible for creating and crafting your purposeful life by choosing moments that are fulfilling rather than simply filling in the moments – this is the difference between living and existing.

When you're busy spinning plates, it's difficult to get a true reflection on your life. If you're in the frame, you're not able to see the big picture. Sometimes it takes someone else to hold up a mirror or requires stepping out of the frame to provide clarity on your surroundings and identity. More importantly, it reveals opportunities for action.

Living or Existing

Over the years, my husband Jon and I had drifted off course from our original vision. Partly living, partly existing, juggling a busy family life with stressful, unfulfilling work, regularly getting home late exhausted, we'd miss out on precious time with our children, Holly and Eddie. Time we'd never get back.

One night in the summer of 2016, it struck me that we'd been merely filling in the moments for years. We'd been caught up in the waves of London city life, riding the daily commuting surf alongside many others, not stopping to question decisions, just moving with the flow of the tide, winding down in the evenings, drinking alcohol, numbing our lives even further. But somehow, on this one evening, things were different.

If you'd been there, as Jon walked in from a long day's work, you'd have seen that something in him had shifted, perhaps even departed. He'd become a lifeless shadow of a man, lost in a thick fog, at the point of burnout – greyed out, ashen. This was Jon, but I barely recognised him. The stress of his job was taking its toll on his health. Our lifestyle had to change. Now.

How had I not spotted it sooner? I felt awful recalling that one of his work colleagues had tried to warn me a few months back of his concern for Jon, but I'd simply shrugged it off. Surrounded by people all burning the candle at both ends, we were no different from our friends and colleagues. This was just what had to be done. It was the norm to work this way, the compromise you made living in London.

As a working mum, I'd been led to believe it was possible to be, do and have it all. We'd been trying to strike the balance that others appeared to have and we'd been pulling it off too. But had we really? Looking closer, it appeared we hadn't. Both at differing points of burnout, to continue like this was simply not sustainable. It wasn't just Jon who'd been existing in such a thick fog. I too had been blinded to our situation. However, it was Jon who was really struggling, barely treading water, and I felt an intense drive to do something to save him, to save us, but in a sustainable way that would prevent us both from drowning!

I knew we needed to change our lifestyle and adopt a new way of life. Seeing our reality made me take responsibility for our future; I couldn't contemplate living the rest of my life without Jon by my side. The path we'd taken wasn't the right one. We had to choose a new path. This was the moment I took control, switched off autopilot, stopped existing and started living.

I resigned from my job to focus all my energy on planning a change in our lifestyle. Despite having a clear why and purpose, I lacked clarity on the plan but trusted I'd figure it out. As it happened, the universe began to work its magic sooner than anticipated. On my train journey home, I spotted an ad in the London freesheet *Metro* for a property auctions seminar on 9 September 2016. Intrigued, I attended it and subsequently enrolled in a year-long property investment training course. This marked the beginning of a new path to explore.

On 30 September 2016, armed with my why, purpose and a clear plan for change, I focused on building a business that would liberate Jon from a stressful, unfulfilling job in the City. Setting a target date for his departure for three years hence, although distant, provided Jon with hope. Seeing an end in sight, a weight lifted and his health started to improve.

A New Way of Life

So, what happened three years later, on 30 September 2019? Did my unwavering focus, determination and commitment to the purpose-driven plan pay off? Yes, it worked. Just three days after my planned target, Jon exited his job. Through the new property business I'd established, I'd crafted a new sustainable lifestyle for our family. While it didn't entirely replace Jon's income, upon reviewing our financial situation in detail, we realised we didn't require as much as we'd been pursuing all those years.

If you're curious about Jon's current status, he's doing really well. However, you might have trouble tracking him down, as he now prioritises what truly matters to him: family, health, charity, community and sport. He's also assumed responsibility for managing the running of the property business, enabling me to concentrate on coaching and podcasting.

On reflection, we'd lost control and focus, and needed to realign with the plan we'd made over 20 years ago in our early twenties. While our values had remained mostly unchanged, we'd neglected some and been living in conflict with others. Having lost sight of what really mattered to us, we'd been swept up into living out other people's dreams, expectations and intentions.

Jon's declining health had acted as the catalyst propelling us into living with intention and purpose, urging us to reassess priorities, clarify our values, be of greater service to others, leave a legacy and invest in our personal growth. Ultimately, it offered us a wonderful new perspective on life.

There had been no focus on purpose. We'd been existing, not truly living. When we realigned our work with our values to build a new lifestyle, everything else started to fall into place. With a purpose, a plan and a clear why, we brought more meaning into our life, which prevented us from simply filling in the moments to instead create fulfilling moments. Having switched off the autopilot, Jon and I now spend our days as we choose, with intentional action. As proud midlife beginners, from this rejuvenated, enlightened perspective, we adopted the phrase 'It's never too late to...'

For me, 'It's never too late to...' meant I was determined to fulfil a long-standing desire to write a book. Seeking guidance from various coaches, I embarked on a creative writing session in January 2022. In that session, I visualised my maternal grandfather, George, sharing captivating wartime stories with me by the fireside – a cherished childhood memory. The concept was that these stories would contain hidden life lessons that would help the reader navigate their future with purposeful intention. With this inspired vision, I began writing 'The Book'.

However, grappling with writer's block two months later, I enlisted the help of another coach to overcome the limiting belief that I lacked the ability to do justice to our story and meet George's exacting standards as a professional playwright and novelist, despite him no longer being alive to judge me.

Through a mindset coaching session, I engaged in an imaginary dialogue with George. Encouraged by his supportive words, this session helped me recognise that my podcasting work was essentially a continuation of George's career in broadcasting, and that writing 'The Book' was a natural progression. With renewed confidence, I resumed writing.

From Beyond the Grave

Goodbye, Ruth

We'd been planning a garden celebration for my grandmother's 90th birthday in June. Sadly, it was not to be. She had collapsed and been taken to hospital. When I arrived at her bedside, hearing me speak, she roused herself for a brief conversation. Nothing could have prepared me for this moment. What do you say to someone who's been so important to you for so many years? Tears expressed what my words could not. I explained that I'd be back with Mum soon. We blew each other kisses and she closed her eyes.

My grandmother and I shared a special bond, more like friends – so much so I called her by her first name, Ruth. She was a true artist of many crafts: watercolour, embroidery and knitting. With love, she hosted, entertained and created stunning gardens for many to enjoy. My earliest memory is of us, hand in hand, slowly making our way back down the narrow lane to her thatched cottage from the village shop. We'd pause to admire the beautiful country garden flowers and Ruth would crouch down by my side to patiently teach me each of their names.

Her eyes were closed, but feeling her grip and sensing she could still hear us, my mum, brother and I sang to her and shared memories of the wonderful moments we'd spent together. We thanked her for all the love she'd given us, shared how much joy she'd brought to the world, and acknowledged our gratitude for how she'd always been there for anyone who needed her. It was heartbreaking yet beautiful and I'm so grateful to have been there, right by her side when, hand in hand, we said our final goodbye.

George (Precious)

Several months later, in December 2022, my mother and I were going through Ruth's various possessions. She hadn't kept much from her almost 90 years of life: a shelf or two of novels and books about birds, gardening and artists; a collection of photographs; her own beautiful artwork; some pieces of jewellery; a few bundles of knitting wool; and an old, battered box with 'George (Precious)' written on the side in my grandmother's writing. This box had been hidden for decades. I carefully unpacked the items, feeling as though I'd just stumbled upon the most valuable treasure ever.

Inside, I found a notebook with 11 handwritten short stories dated February 1943–May 1944, photographs taken inside prisoner of war (POW) camps, a military identity card, a prison number inscribed on a metal tag, and a bundle of letters and telegrams. Then, from deep inside the box, I unearthed a notebook that my grandfather, George Fleming Kerr, had kept as a POW during World War Two (WW2). On the cover, it read: *Commonplace Scrapbook September '39–April '45* and on the inside cover, 'Being notes, reminiscences, impressions, criticism, commentary and work in progress or unfinished made at Eichstätt, Tittmoning, Laufen in Bavaria and Warburg in Westphalia'.

As I flicked through the pages of tiny ink handwriting, it fell open at this entry:

30 September 1942
Proposal to write 'Way of Life' to meet the need for a planned life, to meet every circumstance of life, every facet of living.

Stunned, I was taken aback. A planned life? How extraordinary to read these words, given that purposeful, planned living is exactly what I talk about every day as the focus of my coaching work. 'Have a Purpose. Have a Plan. Focus on Why' is how I end every single podcast episode. My mind was racing, overwhelmed by the potential significance of this scrapbook's discovery.

As with my grandmother, Ruth, I'd also called George by his first name. My earliest memories are of the times I spent with both of them. With unconditional love, each taught me different things about life. A Stoic, socialist, pacifist, philosopher, existentialist, humanist and vegetarian, George was witty with an incisive mind and wide interests. He always put a positive spin on life, stating that the future would be 'lovely', that life was 'graceful'.

Together we'd watch Shakespeare plays and read books, critiquing them afterwards. From a very young age, George taught me not to accept things at face value but to enquire further, how to really listen, understand what interested people, and how to ask great questions. In the shade of the apple trees, we'd spend hours discussing the meaning of life, his time in Australia or just listening to birdsong. In all my time with George, never once did he fail to meet my curiosity for life.

My grandparents shaped my formative years, particularly teaching me how to appreciate and recognise the beauty found in nature, art and literature. But it was George who taught me how to love maths and science in equal measure, and who encouraged me to reflect on what I'd just read or learned to see how it could be applied in my own life. An early adopter of technology, he bought me a word processor, an extravagant gift that he referred to as 'an essential weapon'.

During my teenage years, I lived with my grandparents, and George, having attended my school parents' evenings, would offer reflections with recommended actions to help enhance my performance. I'd only just finished my linguistics degree when his life came to an end in 1996. Coincidentally, I was 21, the same age as George had been when he'd begun writing his Commonplace Scrapbook.

Series of Coincidences

Just 11 months after conceiving the idea to write 'The Book', by incorporating extracts from George's Commonplace Scrapbook, I'd finally obtained the missing jigsaw piece I needed for our collaboration to succeed. George's presence had been his greatest gift to me. His early influence shaped me and directed my path. I wish he were alive now so we could talk more about the meaning and purpose of life. How different this book would've been with his physical, conscious input and what a wonderful guest he would've been on my podcast. Sadly, it wasn't to be. Or was it?

Still sifting through my grandmother's possessions from her loft and looking for one of George's manuscripts, on 15 April 2023, coincidentally on what would've been his 105th birthday, my mum and I found a microcassette tape in an envelope labelled 'Amy & George 1990'. Pressing play, it was me, aged 15, interviewing George, aged 72, about his experiences as a POW. I was speechless. Tears of joy ran down my face. I couldn't believe it. This was serendipity at play. I'd been searching for one thing and found yet another treasure.

Picture the scene: Ruth is in the kitchen prepping dinner, George and I are in the lounge of their house in Stratford-upon-Avon. The quality of a home recording made more than three decades ago isn't great; however, if you listen to the podcast *Focus on WHY* (referred to as FOW going forward), episode 350, 'Chronicles of Captivity', you can clearly hear what we're saying. Here's an extract from that conversation:

AMY: You were a prisoner of war for five years in Germany. How has that affected you and your attitudes towards Germans?

GEORGE: I came out feeling pretty tolerant, really. Because I think a prisoner of war is a fairly balanced character.

AMY: And when you were in a POW camp, did other people have the same opinions as you?

GEORGE: They were very conventional opinions people have because we were in an officers' camp, and an officer's duty, according to king's or queen's regulations, is to escape. But that was my last thought because I thought that extremely perilous and might endanger my life. And I didn't think I owed my country that kind of sacrifice. So I'm a fairly unheroic soldier. But then if you have conscription, which is compulsory enlisting, then you're going to get people like me.

AMY: Were there many people like you or did most people want to escape?

10

GEORGE: A great number of people wanted to escape, because they had left their newly married wives back in England, and mostly they wanted to get through the wire.

AMY: And you weren't married?

GEORGE: I wasn't married, and I didn't have that kind of…

AMY: Responsibility?

GEORGE: Or envy or jealousy or suspicion.

AMY: How old were you?

George: About 20.

AMY: So, you were very young. So, you weren't quite sure what was going on?

GEORGE: No, not at all. At 20, do you know anything? You just play it by ear.

AMY: So, if you didn't escape, does this mean that you betrayed your country?

GEORGE: Some people will think so, yes. I don't. I think you must have your own judgement and assessment of circumstances. For instance, the Germans, whose great motto was 'Befehl ist Befehl', 'orders are orders', they tended to obey any order they were given, hence the atrocities. And when they were called up for war crimes after the war, their defence was, 'I was told to do it. I couldn't disobey an order.' But I think people must be in a position to disobey an order if they think it's an unlawful order or an idiotic order. And I thought that it was idiotic for me to be ordered to climb through several thicknesses of barbed wire with a searchlight on me and machine guns trained on me. It was a silly order.

AMY: So, you're not patriotic in any way?

GEORGE: In any way? Of course I am. My roots are in Great Britain, but I'm not patriotic to the point of folly. It was Dr Johnson, I think, who said that 'patriotism was the last refuge of a scoundrel' and I tend to agree with that.

AMY: How were you treated? Were you treated badly?

GEORGE: Well, we never knew what was going to happen. They tended to take hostages. They tended to do certain purges and shoot people. They tended to parade you at three in the morning and you wondered why. Then they marched you off to another place altogether, a barn, and put you in it; you didn't know if you were going to be shot there. In fact, it was retaliation for something that had been done to German prisoners in Jersey and the Channel Islands. And so, you never knew which way they were going to bite or jump, and that was for five years, so you'd get a bit tense really. You didn't know how long it was going to last but you had written home to your family saying, 'I'll see you in Canada if necessary. Don't wait for me in Great Britain if we are invaded,' and so on. I also reassured my family. I said, 'Don't worry, I shan't try to escape.' That meant that I would get back alive at least but join them elsewhere if they felt that they were in danger in the country.

RUTH: Most of your friends who tried to escape were shot.

GEORGE: Oh, yes.

AMY: Did you get letters back from them [family]?

GEORGE: Oh yes, they came back. They were all censored, of course, but we got letters. We were only allowed to write a letter a month, I think it was, or a letter a fortnight. But it was a fairly interesting monastic life for me at that age. It was like a university because they had a small library. Eventually they got a bigger library from the Swiss Red Cross. Then you could study anything really and I did an external London BA and I learned and passed exams in Spanish and French. I learned to play the flute. I learned to dabble at water-painting. I did a lot of writing and did a lot of reading. I did acting and it was a very rounded life. I played cricket when we had a ball. Rounded, yeah.

AMY: It was OK, really?

GEORGE: Well, no, people still died from suicide. I thought it was OK. I also knew these were the happiest days of your life, but I was certainly not in the majority on that. I mean they thought I was daft.

AMY: Who thought you were daft?

GEORGE: Well, I was unmarried. The other prisoners, especially the married ones, I suppose, would keep getting 'Dear John' letters from their wives, you see. 'I've met this Polish officer', and I hadn't got that problem. I liked it. It was like a university. But of course, I was hungry, it was cold and it was miserable. You had no friends apart from in prison. But the thing you noticed was, and I spent five years there, I only saw one fight in my life.

AMY: Really?

GEORGE: In all that time. You learned to live. I can live with anybody at close quarters. You notice their idiosyncrasies and funny habits and so on. And you may hate them, but you control it.

AMY: So, you think everyone should have five years in prison, then?

GEORGE: I think it wouldn't be bad that, monastic, yeah, especially if there's a library, but of course it doesn't suit people who are not academic.

AMY: How did you get the flute?

GEORGE: Well, it came from the Red Cross.

AMY: Do you play now?

GEORGE: No, I've never played since. I wasn't any good. I took lessons from a boy who learned from Marcel Moyse, who was a great flautist, but it was just a way of passing time I suppose. But more importantly, I wrote too in there. I knew what I was going to do all the time.

Listening back to this recording, and knowing that after the war George went on to spend a lifetime writing, I was particularly struck by these words: 'I knew what I was going to do all the time.' Even though he said he didn't 'know anything' aged 20, he'd learned how to live, understood what he could control and spoke of his understanding of destiny and the meaning of life. He'd had a purpose, a plan and a clarity of focus throughout his POW years and beyond.

However, 'I knew what I was going to do all the time' held another meaning for me. I too had also known what I was going to do! Discovering the scrapbook and tape felt as if the universe was aligning to support the creation of 'The Book', guided by my beloved grandfather. This series of extraordinary, serendipitous coincidences felt like a reunion with George in a beautiful and unexpected way. Despite his physical absence, his presence remained and I wondered after all these years what more he could teach me about life from beyond the grave. A lesson about the nature of coincidence itself, perhaps?

In August 2023, I received an email from a PhD student studying Australian television plays (1956–1970) who'd identified George as a key figure. Having read one of my blogs about George, he'd tracked me down to generously share an extensive collection of his scripts, one of which was a play for Australian TV called *She'll Be Right* about a POW struggling with survivor's guilt. He'd also written this in French as a radio play, which was selected as Australia's entry for the 1961 Prix Italia.

Is it a coincidence that more than half a century later someone on the other side of the world should also be writing about George at exactly the same time as me? Wondering what George would think about this series of coincidences, I realised we'd already discussed this topic 30 years ago while I was still at university.

> **Extract from George's letter to me dated 10 November 1993**
> We tend to react at the astonishing fact of a 'coincidence'. But surely what would be really remarkable would be if – considering the millions and millions of possible combinations of events – if there were NEVER any such coincidences.

A series of meaningful coincidences that seem to defy logical explanation and hint at deeper interconnectedness between events and inner lives is what Swiss psychiatrist Carl Jung termed synchronicity. When synchronicity and serendipity converge, the universe aligns perfectly to bring about an outcome in a way you might never have anticipated, creating magical moments of insight, discovery and life-changing opportunities.

Perhaps now you can appreciate how discovering George's Commonplace Scrapbook inspired and propelled forward my purpose-focused journey to write 'The Book', as he holds a special place in my heart and soul, continuing to guide me from beyond.

Chronicles of Captivity

Before proceeding, I need to share some important disclaimers. I'm not a qualified psychologist, neuroscientist, organisational behaviour specialist or a war historian and neither is this book about a WW2 hero. For if it were, I would've written about my paternal grandfather, Major General Walter Morland Hutton, CB, CBE, DSO, MC, MA, known to one and all as 'Fearless Jim'.

In *Tanks Across the Desert – The War Diary of Jake Wardrop* (Forty 1981), Fearless Jim is described as 'one of the greatest guys who ever joined the Army. He was always well up in his tank giving orders on the wireless in a nice, pleasant voice, just like the announcer reading the news. The lads would have done anything for him and gone anywhere with him – if he had said we were going to make a frontal attack on the gates of hell, they would have been off like a shot.'

Therefore I am the much-loved granddaughter of both an outstanding professional soldier and an ordinary conscript; one spoke directly with Churchill, the other spoke of him. One was injured several times, yet always returned to the front line; the other was not keen to fight at all, and was captured early on. Yet it's because of the action of a 'fairly unheroic soldier' that this particular book has been shaped. If George hadn't spent years in captivity compiling his scrapbook, I wouldn't be able to tell you his story of courage, autonomy and strength of purpose.

With those disclaimers declared, as a qualified coach, experienced podcast host and as George's granddaughter, my expertise lies in sharing what I, and many others, have gained through years of personal experience: the difference between living with and without purpose.

Having left Merchant Taylors' School in Crosby in 1935, George pursued a career in accountancy to please his father. In 1940, aged just 22, he began his five years of captivity as a POW never knowing for certain what would happen, if the next moment might be his last, and armed only with his school education, an inquisitive mind and a developing appreciation for the arts. However, it was this period of confinement that ultimately taught George how to set himself free from a 'Way of Life' he'd previously felt destined to live. He used his period of imprisonment to grow. Learning and crafting his purpose, he broadened his mind and horizon through reading and writing extensively, finding great solace from within the world of literature, nature and music.

Two years later, in 1942, aged 37, Austrian neurologist and psychiatrist Viktor E Frankl began his three years of captivity in the Nazi concentration camps having had his ready-to-publish manuscript confiscated. In *Man's Search for Meaning* (1959), Frankl stated that 'those who knew that there was a task waiting for them to fulfil were most apt to survive' and attributed his ability to 'survive the rigours of the camps' to his 'deep desire to write this manuscript anew'. Drawing from his professional insights, experiences and academic knowledge, Frankl may have lost his manuscript but he'd retained a profound understanding of the significance of purpose and the distinction between what he could and couldn't control.

I want to stress that I'm not in any way equating Frankl's captivity in the concentration camps to George's as a POW. They're not comparable. However, there are parallels between how Frankl and George dealt with their respective circumstances as both men documented their experiences spent in captivity; Frankl in *Man's Search for Meaning*, George in his Commonplace Scrapbook.

Both recorded the meanings behind their observations to provide clear insights as to how they activated their own mental liberation. Throughout their differing personal narratives of survival, it's clear they shared the mindset that as an individual it's your responsibility to shape your own meaning of life. That while life tests you, you have a choice in how you respond. This choice of how to respond is what I refer to in my coaching work and podcasts as Reflection with Action. The action you take that follows your reflection is critical in achieving a life rich in meaning, fulfilment and purpose.

A Later Chronicler

By calling it a Commonplace Scrapbook, George blended both the style of a journal with that of a commonplace book in which you capture information from a variety of sources that informs your view of the world. Including moments of inspirational wisdom and writings from philosophers, poets, authors, even emperors, woven alongside his own thoughts and reflections, his collection marks the beginnings of him crafting and honing his writing skills in preparation for his future career. In essence, he shares his innermost thoughts and reflections on life while living in captivity in his early twenties. You can see the makings of the man he was to become, and the man I would come to know many decades later.

Spanning a six-year period, George's Commonplace Scrapbook begins in the safety of his home in Southport, England, listening to an unimaginable war unfold on the radio. He documents his feelings about becoming a conscripted soldier, his doubts heading into war, travelling towards the front, evading capture and his surrender. Then having been marched across France into Germany, he writes of his time held captive as a POW for five years in four different camps. He often refers to his two brothers, also displaced by the war to other parts of the world, and shares memories of their time as a family.

His scrapbook wasn't intended for publication in its original form. After all, it was just his own personal and profound observations, reflections, musings, dreams, truths, doubts and fears. However, George may have used his scrapbook as a source reference because after the war, with permission to go on indefinite leave under the category 'unposted', George accepted a job offer for the 1946 film *The Captive Heart,* starring Michael Redgrave, as 'technical-cum-atmospheric adviser-cum-extra'. He was instrumental in ensuring the film's accuracy in depicting POW life, and even had a few spoken lines.

The scrapbook also likely aided in writing his two plays based on WW2: *A Month of Sundays,* which was screened on the BBC in 1952, and *She'll Be Right* (1961), screened on Australian TV. Each play is a reminiscence and a noble lament for the millions who lost their lives during the war. Both feature George's own prison number 1536, personal family names for characters and his own insights, habits and virtues are reflected in the dialogue. Characters portray emotions experienced by the POWs: envy, jealousy, suspicion, melancholy, depression, hope, guilt, desire, as well as values of duty, responsibility, fairness, equality and a fear of death.

A Month of Sundays centred around themes of freedom, food, and trust: the perils involved in attempting to escape, the need to receive a parcel containing a crucial part to fix their hidden 'canary' (code for wireless), their desperate hunger, and the wariness of new POWs possibly being German spies. George shared how trust had to be earned over time. The title, *A Month of Sundays* (meaning an extremely long time), is a great metaphor for not being able to escape an interminable situation.

> ### Extract from an article George wrote
> In the play, Calthrop, Burdett and Parkinson are essentially unheroic figures; in real life they were what we were pleased to call 'good prisoners' – not good in the sense that they gave the Germans a great deal of trouble by persistent escape attempts, but good because they had learned to live for years at almost point-blank range with half a dozen others. They had managed somehow to preserve their balance and seemed likely to emerge from behind the wire with their sanity intact and their sense of humour, if anything, improved. Sometimes, of course, their humour failed them and their neighbours seemed intolerably near. This nearness, and how the prisoners tried to make it tolerable, is the subject of the play.
>
> On our return home, we prisoners were astonished to find that people were sorry for us. For our part, we felt only relief; it had been a long sentence and we had survived. We knew that others had met lonely deaths on the wire or in the country lying between the 'kriegie' [POW] and home. Although *A Month of Sundays* tells of those who survived, it remembers the few who did not.

Although he used the scrapbook for his own benefit, I also believe it had been kept safe all these years so that, together, you and I could learn, understand and question what can be achieved through living a life of purpose, whatever our circumstances. In his scrapbook entry on 25 March 1945, writing as if directly addressing an audience, George makes specific reference to a 'later chronicler'.

> Such was the past which these places could remember, a past of which little evidence was left in the valley along the plain. Now and for five years, the Kriegsgefangenenlager *[POW camp]* was to stand there, a building we were to regard as our home. Doubtless it too would contribute something to history, but a later chronicler must speak of this. Doubtless by then the camps would have disappeared; but the rivers would be running yet and the blizzard blowing at Dössel. Let us go in then, out of the blizzard. Let us look at some of these prison camps.

The scrapbook then held one further purpose: to lead me to become the 'later chronicler' who 'must speak of this' as no one else has read this scrapbook. It has to be me. After all these years, my grandfather is speaking to me again.

The Book's Purpose

So, through intergenerational collaboration, my grandfather's scrapbook, together with my Focus on Why Framework, becomes our combined legacy to form *Focus on Why: Create a purposeful way of life.* In sharing George's abridged chronicles of captivity during 20th-century war-torn Europe, you'll witness his physical and existential journey of life and death, freedom and captivity, and destiny and purpose.

This book will empower you to craft your own purposeful life through this blend of my grandfather's scrapbook with wisdom shared from podcasting conversations and my personal experiences and insights as a coach.

The Focus on Why Framework is designed to challenge the authenticity of your current lifestyle, and provides practical, creative Reflection with Action exercises to reinforce learnings from each of the nine steps.

As you navigate the many challenges and transitions of life, you may find this book becomes a lifelong companion. Prepare to venture on a journey of self-discovery, encountering timeless, universal yet deeply personal themes essential to modern-day living with an emphasis on love and compassion for humanity. What purpose do you envision for yourself? What impact and legacy do you aim to create?

Regardless of where you find yourself in life, the Focus on Why Framework transcends age, life stage or circumstance to offer a roadmap through each of life's transitions to create a sustainable, purposeful lifestyle.

The Focus on Why Framework:
Purpose, Plan and Focus

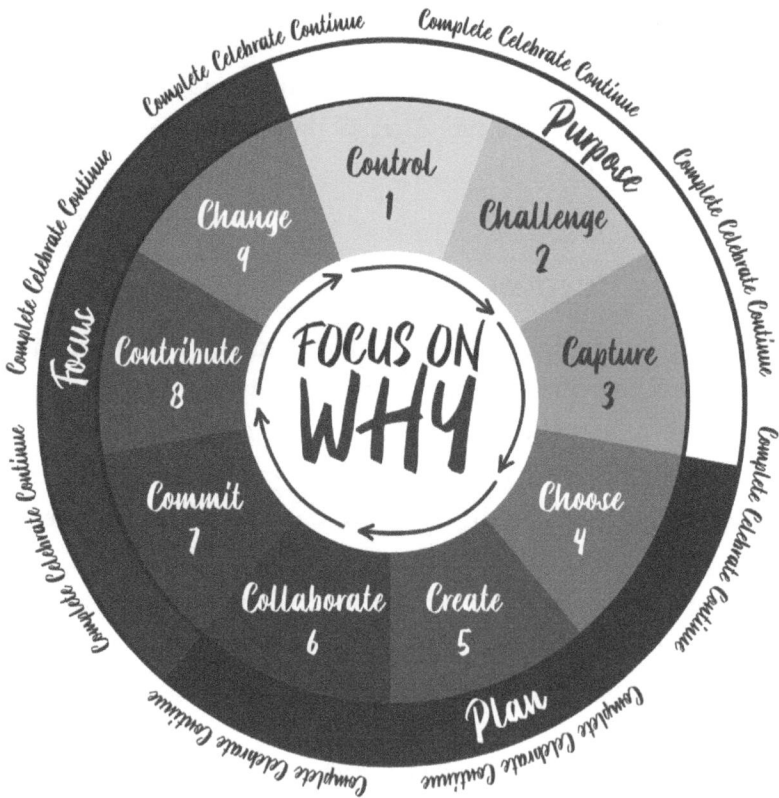

There are three parts to the Framework: Purpose, Plan and Focus.

Part 1: Purpose – comprising three actionable steps – **Control, Challenge and Capture** – centres on your perception and understanding of the world. Serving as your guiding light, infusing clarity, passion and authenticity into your actions, purpose offers deliberate direction and significance to your intentions, empowering you to create a positive impact, contribute meaningfully and experience fulfilment.

Have a Purpose
Step 1: Control the controllables
Step 2: Challenge the status quo
Step 3: Capture what matters

Part 2: Plan – comprising three actionable steps – **Choose, Create and Collaborate** – revolves around your decision making and action taking. A well-structured plan provides the necessary route to achieve your purpose-driven aspirations, breaking down your intentions into manageable milestones.

Have a Plan
Step 4: Choose your actions
Step 5: Create and craft a plan
Step 6: Collaborate to amplify impact

Part 3: Focus – comprising three actionable steps – **Commit, Contribute and Change** – centres on your commitment to a chosen path. As your life evolves and changes, so does your purpose, shaping your intentional and purposeful journey.

Focus on Why
Step 7: Commit wholeheartedly with unwavering focus
Step 8: Contribute to create positive ripple effects
Step 9: Change with your evolving purpose

Use the framework to craft your own unique life of purpose with a focus on what really matters. Work through each of the steps in order from 1 to 9. As you progress through them, be prepared to allocate dedicated time for the Reflection with Action exercises, which are designed to facilitate growth, self-awareness and habit formation. After completing them, embrace the Celebrate and Continue exercises to acknowledge all your achievements and any lessons learned. This self-assessment promotes self-approval and self-appraisal. Once completed, move on to the next step.

Are you ready to start a unique adventure? Then your journey begins here.

PART I
PURPOSE

Have a Purpose
Step 1: Control the controllables
Step 2: Challenge the status quo
Step 3: Capture what matters

Purpose is the overarching intention that guides your direction in life. Your why is the emotional significance you assign to your purpose. Before diving into crafting a plan and setting the course for your lifelong journey of purpose, it's essential to have a deep understanding of, and a strong connection to, your why. As purpose emerges from authenticity, it requires you to strip away any facades to reveal your true essence. This entails authentically understanding who you are rather than moulding yourself to fit in with societal norms or others' expectations.

Step 1: Control

Control the controllables: while navigating life's challenges, gracefully accept and liberate yourself from what you can't control to take control of what you can.

What can't you control? Other people's thoughts, feelings and actions, past events, the passage of time, weather, natural disasters, pandemics, ageing, death and genetic predispositions. You also have limited control over future outcomes, your environment and, through your communication, influence on others. What can you control? Your perspective. This includes: choices, decisions, thoughts, beliefs, behaviours, responses, actions, habits, routines, boundaries, effort and attitude.

When you experience a moment in your life, you intuitively assign a meaning to it, either consciously or unconsciously, based upon your values, beliefs, perceptions, interpretations, experiences and emotions. The secondary subjective meaning you choose then leads to how you respond to that moment through your thoughts, behaviour, the choices you make and subsequently the actions you take. This sequence continues. This is how life unfolds.

On occasion, you may unwittingly relinquish control by letting others control you and dictate your actions, or forget you have a choice in the meaning you assign to the moment and get swept up with emotion. Be mindful of reclaiming control by assuming responsibility for your choices, actions and beliefs. Being aware of what you have limited control over and letting go of what you can't control frees you to focus on what you can.

Reality is focused on objective, factual and unchangeable aspects of the world and your existence. The laws of nature, the physical universe, physical entities, events and phenomena all exist independently of your thoughts, perceptions and beliefs. However, your own reality is shaped by your subjective perceptions influenced by senses, cognitive processes, emotions, memories, beliefs, experiences, perspectives and societal constructs. This is how individuals can each interpret their reality in diverse ways as they reflect a unique blend of these influences.

Millions of pieces of information flood your senses every moment and are all filtered by areas in the brain. With the conscious mind's limited processing capacity, vast amounts of information get deleted, generalised and distorted, filtering out what it deems unnecessary allowing only important details, but also allowing irrelevant details through. It's not a perfect system!

How does the brain discern what's important? Sometimes it makes mistakes, however, it does learn through where you apply your focus, essentially through both reflection and action. Your actions shape the filters influencing your perception, thereby perpetuating the cycle. Daily, you filter information based on beliefs, values, experiences and memories. What remains forms your understanding and appreciation of the world, shaping your unique map of reality and how you perceive information.

This is how you see life through a completely different lens to anyone else in the world. Within this unique reality, there are elements you believe to be true, aspects you know, concepts you're aware of but don't fully understand, and then there's an entire realm of existence that lies beyond your perception and model of the world: all the things you don't know you don't know.

Essentially, you control your reflections and actions, shaping who you are and what you do. This means you have control over choosing your desires, intentions, aspirations and ultimately your purpose. This is what to focus on in life. Taking control entails autonomy of your values, needs and desires. It involves taking ownership of your life to shape every moment. Any struggles you encounter will be made more difficult when you try to control the uncontrollable. True freedom emerges when you let go of what's beyond your control.

Freedom and responsibility are essential components for achieving purpose and fulfilment as they complement one another. Freedom enables self-expression, encourages choice, innovation, creativity and personal growth, allowing you to think differently and take risks. Responsibility ensures accountability for your actions and choices, guiding you to live with ethical and moral principles.

Stoic philosopher Epictetus referred to it as the 'reasoned choice' (see Holiday & Hanselman 2016). George applied this wisdom to assist with the mental clarity, courage and resilience he needed to manage uncertainty during his five years of imprisonment. Detaching himself from external circumstances beyond his control, he focused on the inner resilience and strength of his own thoughts and actions to liberate himself from emotional turmoil. Finding meaning from his experiences, he crafted his purposeful 'Way of Life'.

Despite the confinement of lockdown being so limiting, the pandemic actually provided me with a large degree of freedom. By using the wonderful medium of podcasting, I connected virtually with people all over the world, and was able to shine a light on their purpose. When speaking with my guests on my podcast, *Focus on WHY*, inevitably the conversations touch on the importance of freedom. What's interesting is that the type of freedom each person seeks differs and is invariably linked to other elements. Freedom is partnered with creativity, work, exploration, love, choice, flexibility, opportunity, acceptance, independence, kindness, time and curiosity. What type of freedom do you seek?

In FOW 146, 'Points of Impact', keynote speaker and leadership trainer Tim Durkin expressed how the writings of Epictetus, Seneca and Marcus Aurelius remain highly appropriate for our volatile, uncertain, complex and ambiguous (VUCA) times today. Tim considers the most important book to read is Frankl's *Man's Search for Meaning* and part of the reason he'd been able to both see and have a 'lot of silver linings in the pandemic' was because he applied Frankl's freedom of choice. Describing it as the 'last of the human freedoms', Frankl wrote, 'Man is capable of changing the world for the better if possible and of changing himself for the better if necessary. Every human being has the freedom to change at any instant.'

Connecting to the reality of what you can control while accepting what you can't, let's address self-talk. Considering you'll spend the rest of your life with your inner dialogue, wouldn't it be simpler if you took charge of what you tell yourself? Whether you're conscious of it or not, your language, both internally and externally, significantly impacts your life. How do you speak to yourself?

Along with your other sub-personalities or inner selves, your inner critic is trying to keep you safe by pointing out all your faults and mistakes. But equally, this self-talk can cause great suffering in the process. Knowing that these voices aren't necessarily speaking the truth and mastering your internal dialogue will give you back your power. Separate out the voices by giving them names and acknowledge what their specific roles are in keeping you safe. Understand how they're monitoring and policing the rules you've set them to follow and know that you have a choice to believe what they're saying.

My more dominant sub-personalities are all trying to help me achieve my intentions by influencing my thoughts and actions. These include my 'pusher', which drives me to be endlessly busy, along with my 'perfectionist', 'responsible self', 'inner critic', 'protector/controller' and 'pleaser'. But I also see how devastatingly detrimental they can sometimes be, leading me to entertain beliefs of inadequacy, constantly striving to attain perfection or allowing my boundaries to be crossed in prioritising others' needs above my own simply to please them.

In FOW 122, 'Be Kind to Yourself', Kim-Adele Platts (now Randall), who specialises in helping board-level executives lead with impact and humanity, said, 'Unless you learn to be kind to yourself, at some point you'll run out of steam. If you don't learn the lesson, life will repeat itself until you do.' Learn to love and empower yourself to become everything you've ever aspired to be. Pay close attention to the lessons life offers and remember you get to choose and assign the meaning of each moment.

At the root of many challenges is low self-worth. Positive self-talk serves as a powerful tool to becoming more confident, driven, focused, productive, motivated and more purposeful in your actions. When you learn to be kind and love yourself and believe you are good enough even when you fail, you cut through the noise to master the true power of your thinking. It's not the events in your life that define you but how you choose to live your life afterwards. Do you allow disruptions to throw you off course or do you learn from them and adapt?

Jon, Eddie and I were standing at the 19-mile mark with our motivational signs, waiting for Holly to run past, when the phone rang. It was a paramedic informing us that Holly had overheated, collapsed and would be taken to the medical centre. Reassuring us she was OK, he instructed us to head straight there. This wasn't the marathon outcome Holly had trained really hard for.

After she'd recovered a couple of days later, she felt immense disappointment at not having finished. I explained to her that all emotions are good and provide a service, to acknowledge the disappointment and decide whether that was a useful way for her to respond or not. That it was now within her to choose how she felt and she could change the meaning of the event and understand the personal lesson life was offering her to take from the disappointment she was experiencing.

Mindful to emphasise that this was just *my* truth and not *the* truth, I offered my personal reflection on the event. What I'd witnessed on that marathon day was that in a time of need, you're not alone; there are always people who'll love and care for you – some you'll know well and some will remain strangers whose names you'll never know, but they'll always be there. I reminded her of a cross-country race when, aged ten, instead of trying to win, she'd held back to support a struggling friend. Life isn't a competition; it's about collaboration, compassion and love, and this marathon event showed this lesson in abundance. While you can plan and prepare, you can't control the future outcome, the weather or rely on the body to be predictable. But you can choose the meaning of each moment you experience, how you feel and the subsequent action you take.

Your medal from this marathon wasn't going to be one made of metal to only later gather dust, but instead one you get to feel every day, deep inside your heart, knowing you're loved and capable of love and gratitude for others. What a precious gift to receive and give. You didn't need to finish the marathon to prove anything to find or show love – it was already there. What I'd witnessed on that day was a beautiful lesson of love.

Reflecting on her own understanding of the situation, Holly's response was to apply for next year's London marathon, running for St John Ambulance to acknowledge her overwhelming gratitude for the incredible care and support they'd given her and us as a family. A few weeks later, St John Ambulance offered her a place.

George's Scrapbook
September 1939 – 30 March 1940

Throughout these excerpts from George's Commonplace Scrapbook, I'll offer my insights, provide context and shed light on events outside the POW camps as well as include extracts from any correspondence he sent or received. George's scrapbook excerpts and all correspondence will appear in tinted boxes.

On 3 September 1939, Britain officially declared war on Germany, with Parliament passing the National Service (Armed Forces) Act, imposing conscription on all males aged between 18 and 41 to register for service. George was expected to serve his country, and it was around this date that he started keeping his scrapbook, documenting his reflections on the impending change in his own personal circumstances and starting to define his future 'Way of Life'.

George was the youngest of three brothers. John, the eldest, was a doctor who joined the Royal Army Medical Corps, later serving in Cairo, Egypt. Donald, the middle son, formerly a captain in the Royal Army Service Corps, subsequently joined the Royal Air Force to become a pilot officer. Their mother had died when they were young but their father had remarried, and Helen became known fondly as Amie, French for friend. (She was still alive when I was born; I was named in her honour.)

September 1939, Southport

I sit in my stuffy little office and listen to John's portable. Once again the announcer tells of the towns bombed by the Nazi air force: 'Warsaw, Częstochowa, Kraków, Łódź, Lwów...' Kraków hurts most, I don't know why. Perhaps because of its city square or its university, or because of the cathedral which for centuries has watched the coronations and burials of the Polish kings.

This morning German planes again flew over western Poland and bombed Warsaw, Częstochowa, Lwów, Łódź, Kraków...

11 October 1939, Liverpool

My head feels lighter for the hair the Adelphi trimmed me of. But although I have made this first sacrifice to the new way of life, I still cling to the old school scarf Amie knitted for me, to the green overcoat and the green wildfowl pork pie hat.

The poker school drags its way across the length of England and, smoking and coughing, we 18 recruits hurry towards London and our last brief hours of freedom. For if our send-off is not to be glorious, let it be so dirty and mean that we shall remember it for that, and for that only. Let us shut the carriage windows, and smoke, cough and play cards. And when we arrive in the capital of our country, let us eat coarsely in a fish and chip bar.

It was done too suddenly, on impulse. Everyone seemed glad. John helped me to buy some things in Liverpool, amongst them a record for Amie, 'Mr Bach goes to town', a jeu d'esprit, nothing more. So much is that and no more…

December 1939, Aldershot

I am lost in this place. The long physical day puts me into a deep sleep each night. But all this cheerfully bad singing, the hurry and jostle in the canteen, the mass activity whether at drill on the square, in the bath huts, at lunch, or at night in the town, all this cannot be my world forever.

Or if it is so to be, then I want someone else to be in it with me. I feel now that I need never have joined up, that life in England is everywhere else quite normal, and that I am now as forgotten as any drummer boy in the Peninsular War.

Doubts and fear have set in, time is dragging, the environment unfamiliar, with no sense of belonging or feeling of support. George knew this wouldn't be his world forever, but at this point he felt the direction of his life was out of his control. His new reality is unlike anything he's ever experienced. With the drummer boy metaphor, in all the noise and confusion of wartime preparation, he can barely hear his own thoughts.

I phoned Donald at Bulford. His voice was wonderfully reassuring. He has accepted this life and is obviously enjoying it immensely. Of course, as an officer it must be rather fine. Bulford is so very far from Aldershot. I haven't money for the journey nor available time, nor a private car. We are separated by a World War.

Echoing Winston Churchill's sentiment, 'There is no doubt that it is around the family and the home that all the greatest virtues… are created, strengthened and maintained', George feeling alone and lost, reaches out to his brothers – Donald first, then John.

The night drive was exciting. Last week the Canadians had set up a lap record, but in the mud and fog and total darkness I was not anxious to take chances. Indeed I was surprisingly incompetent. I managed to bring the 3-tonner back without casualty but Bill, who was with me, was stiff with terror. He lay back in his seat when we berthed, covering his eyes and saying, 'Oh Gawd, George, oh Gawd!'

John came down to see me yesterday. We dined at the Victoria Hotel. He seemed self-conscious in his 'civvies' amongst so much khaki; but oh how I envied him his civilised appearance. I felt sure he had come as a representative of the family, and I was very grateful. But I knew that it was the whining note of my letters had brought him.

Christmas 1939, Southport

A wonderful leave. The two worlds united again. John is very busy doing the practice for Daddy, while he lies impatiently in plaster and defies a broken back. Everyone went out of their way to make me happy, and succeeded more than they could know. Roaring around Southport in the old Humber, Donald in his officer's uniform, myself a neat and polished cadet, I felt very proud of him and of myself.

I looked twice yesterday at a soldier with B.E.F. *[British Expeditionary Force]* on his shoulder tabs. I am in awe of the man in action. He certainly looked tough and he walked with a swagger.

12 March 1940, Barry Island, Wales
As I am to be a soldier, I may as well be a good one. So I am full of ambition, and working hard. I have a section under my command and I am Officer I/C Sports, Officer I/C Entertainments, Detachment Orderly Officer, President of the Mess Committee *[PMC]*, and Assistant Adjutant. If I'm lucky, I may get a captaincy in two or three months.

Accepting responsibility for his life, the lives of others and the role he must fulfil, George's values of ambition, hard work and pride align him with his work. In accepting what lay beyond his control, he achieved an inner peace and discovered a capacity towards adaptability and resilience.

23 March 1940, Penarth
A lovely dinner last night with 'Horse' and Betty Perkins. I felt I must dramatise the moment, and went into the hotel lounge to write my last letter before going to war. 'Horse' found me there, lost in a wave of self-pity (which I don't feel at all, of course). Self-pity or liqueur brandy.

Documenting events becomes George's way of processing thoughts, feelings, actions and the meaning of the moment. He's yet to understand that his prolific wartime journaling habit will play a key role not only in his mental survival but in the creation of his future fulfilling, purposeful life.

25 March 1940, Barry Island
'Hello. Is that Southport 3821? – Hello John – it's George – yes – I thought I'd phone up – you remember you said I would phone up if – yes – yes – oh fine, thanks – righto, thanks – hello Daddy – yes – yes – pretty soon I think – oh fine, thanks – I don't know – no – yes – you know? – Are you all well? – good – hello Amie – oh fine thanks – yes – no, fine thanks – yes – yes – well I'll have to go now – yes – goodbye – hello Daddy – say goodbye to everyone for me will you? – yes – goodbye – goodbye.'

> **26 March 1940, Ramsgate**
> Two officers, brothers. One of them, at least, proud as a peacock. One brother gets into the carriage, the other stays on the platform, swishing his swagger stick. Embarrassed, we shake hands, say goodbye, absurdly, unnaturally casual. The train moves out, and I lean from the window. We both wave a hand once, and then – Donald turns and is lost to sight.

This beautiful and touching farewell between two brothers represents the difficult moment many experienced saying goodbye to their loved ones during the war. Notice how the entry switches mid paragraph from third person to first person, from detachment to personalisation. Of course he didn't know it then, but this was the last time George and his brother would ever see one another as tragically Donald would indeed be 'lost to sight'.

> **27 March 1940, London**
> Today I saw 'The Wizard of Oz' three times. It is quite charming. A fairy tale, a painted fantasy. Its philosophy is escape? Yes, I suppose so. And it has these faults too: it is unreal, sentimental, ridiculously optimistic. At any rate it is just what this soldier wants at this moment in time, Spring of the 20th Century World War.
>   'Somewhere over the rainbow, way up high,
>   there's a land that I heard of once in a lullaby.'

A philosophy of escape – George escaped the reality of his situation not once but three times! About to head off to war, the message of 'there's no place like home' would've struck a chord. I'm curious as to why he regarded fantasy, sentimentality and optimism as faults; however, having watched this film as a young girl in the 1980s, I recognise we'd watched it through very different filters and circumstances. This entry serves as a grounding reminder that life isn't all rainbows and lullabies, but I can imagine how the film's optimism would've uplifted him during this time of great uncertainty, offering a sense of control over his future, encouraging him to find beauty in the world and to believe that 'the dreams you dare to dream really do come true'. All contributing to the road optimism paves. A yellow brick road, perhaps?

30 March 1940
The train took us through a part of England new to me, the rows and rows of huts at Didcot, the sidings at Swindon. We stared from the windows as the country moved past us; we were gazing for something of beauty that we could take with us and remember, for ever if need be. The gods were good, for spring was budding as we passed through Bath, and the cleanliness and freshness of the historic little town smiled at our youth, and told us we were not forgotten, not entirely alone.

Blisteringly aware of what lay ahead, here's that search for beauty, yet in contrast to his statement about *The Wizard of Oz*, here sentimentality is a necessity, not a fault. Writing from the perspective of his fellow soldiers collectively represents how desperate they all were to hold onto something to treasure in their hearts and minds. The evocative description of rural England is reminiscent of Edward Thomas's 1914 poem 'Adlestrop', which was treasured by Ruth and George.

Control: Reflections with Actions

As meaning emerges from reflection and purpose arises from action, these exercises aim to establish habits supportive of shaping a fulfilling, purpose-driven life.

↗ JOURNALING

George's preferred weapon of choice was the pen. His journaling habit helped him to process his thoughts, feelings and ideas. Establish or maintain the daily practice of writing to capture both the smaller moments and more significant events and experiences. Writing about your experiences provides perspective and clarity, and aids in making informed decisions. Reducing stress and enhancing problem solving, journaling also helps you to remain in the present. By documenting concerns, fears, doubts and achievements, as well as discerning between controllable and uncontrollable factors, journaling helps build an accurate picture of your reality. Effectively externalising your ideas and thoughts onto paper, it also helps you track intentions, visualise your future and improve your written communication skills. Over time, it will reveal growth and learning.

↗ COMMONPLACE SCRAPBOOK

The practice of keeping a commonplace book lends itself to collecting thoughts, sayings, ideas and concepts assembled from various sources that hold particular meaning and resonance for you. Alongside your journal, establish or maintain the lifelong practice of keeping your own commonplace scrapbook in which to retain snippets of seemingly disconnected information, but which together help you to make sense of your thoughts, purposeful intentions and the world. You may want to treat yourself to a special book purely dedicated to capturing inspiration. Like a literary version of a mood board, highly personal and reflecting unique insights and perspectives, it's a brilliant way to record and highlight what you deem most important in life.

➹ Focus on… Meaningful Definitions

After each podcast episode I record, I reflect on what I've heard and learned. Since August 2020, I've focused on one key word each week and written a blog centred on it for my website. Based on the personal experiences that hold significant meaning for you, begin the practice of defining words, recognising how each word contributes to guiding your intentional actions and achieving fulfilment. This Meaningful Definitions exercise will enhance your understanding of how you interpret the meaning of past events and how they influence your future intentions. Focus on… [insert key word here] and then start writing.

Control: Celebrate and Continue

➹ Gratitude and Small Wins

Before continuing to the next step in the framework, I encourage you to celebrate all the wins in your life as it's easy to let them pass by without any formal recognition. At the end of each day, take a moment to acknowledge everything you're grateful for in life. Reflecting on gratitude shifts your focus away from loss or lack to appreciation of what you already have. As part of this practice, recognise any small wins that occurred during the day. Making this a daily habit will reveal abundance and accomplishments not only leaving you feeling grateful but also satisfied as you drift off to sleep.

Step 1: Control – Summary

There will be moments in life when circumstances are beyond your control, where surrendering to the uncontrollable is inevitable. However, you have a choice in how you respond to these events, and you're responsible for how you define your why and your attitude. Recognising what you can and can't control enables you to be more mindful of your reactions and interpretations of events. Liberate yourself from the stress and anxiety of all the things you can't control, leaving you better equipped to adapt to change and ultimately to live a more fulfilled life.

Step 2: Challenge

Challenge the status quo: examine your present lifestyle, question norms and clarify your true identity, assessing whether the beliefs and values you hold are genuinely yours.

Now you have an understanding of what you can and can't control, the next step is to confront the reality of your current lifestyle. Essentially, it's about being honest about how you're living day to day: discerning a difference between facing uncomfortable truths or choosing to accept comfortable lies. To do this, challenge the status quo and evaluate whether your beliefs truly align with your own values to determine if they're serving you. Confronting the reality of your circumstances, choices and the state of the world is essential for your progress and for making well-informed decisions about your life purpose.

Challenge your priorities across all areas of your life. Question whether you're prioritising your health. Examine your desires, aversions, motivations, judgements and impulses. Don't assume that just because something has been done in a certain way in the past, it must continue in the future. Question all the bad habits you maintain simply because it's easier than striving to change them. If you don't actively choose and define your own purpose, others may impose their definitions upon you, shaping your thoughts, beliefs and actions. Are you living your own life purpose or someone else's?

Essential for growth, questions serve as the roots of all learning. Use questions to acquire and expand your knowledge, solve problems, gain deeper insights and dispel confusion. How effective is your questioning? George taught me that asking great questions is an art requiring skill and practice. Powerful questions inspire clarity, action and discovery, as the quality of the question determines its outcome.

As you transition through different stages of life, the questions you ask evolve and change as you contemplate your life purpose. 'What do I want to be when I grow up?' transforms into 'Who am I?' and then to 'Why am I here? What's my purpose? What's the meaning of life?' The journey continues with questions such as 'What's my calling?' and 'Who have I become as a person?' Eventually, you may ponder, 'What value have I added to people's lives?', culminating in the final question, 'What legacy have I left behind?'

At every stage of life, every moment carries significance as your life is shaped by the choices you make and the questions you ask yourself. Are you making the right choices and are you asking the right questions? Keep questioning, and before you act, ask yourself: will this action help me fulfil my purpose?

Are your current choices and actions in alignment with your values and aspirations? Do you sense purpose and meaning in your pursuits? Are you actively engaging in fulfilling activities? If you answered no to any of these questions, take a moment to reflect on what needs to change.

Who is motivating or directing your actions? While seeking guidance from others is sometimes necessary, do you often feel pressured by social or societal norms, family expectations or cultural traditions? Do you seek validation or approval from others when making career or relationship choices? Do you ever experience resentment or regret about your decisions? Do you blame others for the direction of your life? If these resonate with you, it could indicate that you're living your life for others rather than for yourself.

To live authentically, engage in activities that bring you fulfilment or you're passionate about, understand your personal preferences and strengths, embrace your authentic self, trust your intuition, have a strong sense of self-awareness and self-acceptance, and take responsibility for your actions and choices. When you prioritise people in your decision-making process and understand who you can help, the problem you can solve and the impact you can have, you create purposeful, fulfilling work. This work not only solves personal and professional problems but can also have broader, even global, significance. However, it's essential to invest in self-improvement first to effectively help others.

Is this really it? Who am I? Why am I here? What's my purpose and how do I find it? Do I even need to have a purpose in life? What's it all for? What's the purpose of suffering in life? What's my legacy? How can I be happy? How do I achieve a sense of balance in my life and work? What if

I don't know what my why is? As a coach, I encounter clients grappling with these existential questions about identity, purpose, happiness and fulfilment. To address these same enquiries, I embarked on my own quest, and the journey I've undertaken has been an incredibly transformative experience.

After investing 18 months of my time, money and effort into building a networking and property investment training business, I found myself facing disappointment when not much had materialised. As the first lockdown began on 23 March 2020, anticipating a discussion about transitioning our business to an online platform, I had a conversation with my business partner. What actually unfolded during the conversation was unexpected: my partner expressed a change of heart and, after reflecting on what really mattered to him, no longer wished to continue with the business.

The news hit me hard. To say I was devastated is an understatement. However, after a few days' reflection, I realised it was a blessing in disguise. It gave me the opportunity to create what I call a midlife beginning. While property wasn't my passion, podcasting resonated with me deeply. I enjoyed working with the medium, conducting interviews and listening to people's stories. Also, I realised that coaching, having been a part of my life since I was 14 in one way or another, was also my focus.

With the property training business unexpectedly coming to an end, I desperately tried to think what direction to take next. Seeking inspiration and support, I reached out to a few friends, yet deep down I knew it was time to chart my own course, to trust and follow my own intuition. Wrestling with ideas, uncertain about the business I might create, I found myself constantly changing my LinkedIn profile, sometimes up to five times a day for an entire week!

I was at a crossroads, unsure of which path to take. Initially the transition felt daunting and lonely. I grappled with vulnerability, feeling as though everyone was against me and that things weren't going as planned. It was a challenging period. Despite the uncertainty, I trusted that eventually clarity would come in time, and it did. Although my business partner and I parted ways, I believe that when one door shuts, it's often for a good reason, even if that reason isn't immediately evident.

After pausing to reset and refocus on what I could control, I began to envision where I truly wanted to go, what I wanted to achieve and who I really wanted to become. A week later, on April Fools' Day 2020, I woke up with an idea that would totally change my life trajectory, my business and my network. I felt a surge of possibility and new-found strength. I'd opened a new door and was determined to seize the opportunity. Driven by the belief that this idea held immense potential, I became laser focused. While it hasn't quite reached the viral status I'd initially hoped for, it has undoubtedly made its mark globally.

Following that unexpected curveball of a call on the first day of lockdown, I was overwhelmed by a mix of feelings – anxiety, uncertainty, disappointment and anger – and my plans all seemed to unravel before me. It was a true test of my resilience. However, I made a conscious decision to acknowledge all these emotions. The global reset shifting my mindset, I tapped into my superpowers, areas of expertise and genius, took control, assumed responsibility and sprang into action.

Drawing from past experiences of launching businesses, I approached this challenge as the catalyst for the next phase of life and as a timely opportunity to leverage my existing skills to carve out a new path. If the world was undergoing a global reset, I could too. It was time to step out of the shadows, both those cast by others and by myself. I'd been holding back for too long, not unleashing my full potential nor operating in my true area of expertise. It was time to move on, activate my capabilities and embark on this new journey aligned with my passions, talents and values.

So, on 30 April 2020, amid widespread uncertainty, I took the bold step to launch a podcast called *Focus on WHY*. This venture marked a pivotal shift for me – from addressing personal challenges to solving a broader, global issue. It wasn't merely a problem, it was a crisis: an existential crisis of meaning affecting countless individuals. Using the medium of this podcast, I aimed to offer guidance and support to those feeling unfulfilled, particularly those who, like me, were looking to avoid midlife crises and instead focus on midlife beginnings.

My why: Declining health and burnout prompted a full lifestyle reassessment to living sustainably.

My purpose: Shine a light on what's possible when you Focus on Why.

The why is at the heart of every conversation I have with all my coaching clients, and I knew that by creating the podcast, *Focus on WHY*, I could amplify the message of the significance of purpose and meaning in life on a global scale. Now, four years and hundreds of episodes later, the podcast has sparked thousands of positive ripple effects, creating a lasting impact worldwide.

When I ask my podcast guests about their why, they each open their hearts and dig deep to reveal their emotional journeys. With vulnerability and authenticity, they share extraordinary, passionate and, at times, harrowing stories of purpose and transformation breaking through mental and physical barriers. Their narratives serve as powerful motivators, inspiring and encouraging listeners to take positive action and focus on their own why, emphasising the possibility of transformation and the notion that it's never too late to pursue one's passions.

Danny Gray (FOW 36, 'Put Your War Paint On') shared how his personal story about body dysmorphia and lack of confidence disrupted the cosmetics market and opened doors for men across the world. Bullied from the age of ten due to his appearance, combined with a diagnosis of body dysmorphic disorder, Danny found that make-up gave him back his confidence. By sharing why he created the products and how he uses them, not only does Danny help men understand the value and the benefits, but he proves how one purpose-driven person can change an industry and market perception, and create a powerful living legacy.

Despite their differing perspectives and unique reasons, my podcast guests share at least three common traits: they're living, not merely existing; they didn't 'find' their why, they actively created it; and they constantly question and evolve their sense of purpose. When you unite your passion with a clear purpose and a plan, and take full responsibility for your actions while focusing on your why, that's when you recognise what it will take to bring your vision to life. Whether your aspirations are business related or personal, your why is inherently unique. However, please don't wait for ill health or a disaster to act as the catalyst for your transformation towards building a purposeful life! Take control, take decisive action and assume responsibility for shaping your future now.

'That was the moment where I dared to challenge my status quo,' said Dr Joanna Martin in FOW 308, 'Mission Critical', pinpointing exactly when all her unconscious decisions guided her to living, working and embodying her soulful purpose today. 'Why did you choose to be here? For what purpose? What is it that your soul wants to experience, express and perhaps even change in the world? What's your light that you're here to shine?' Having answered these critical questions herself, now, as an architect and accelerator of change, Jo encourages others to address them, ensuring her mission to unleash the bold, grassroots leadership of one million women worldwide succeeds: 'What we need as an indefatigable resource is the ability to be kind to ourselves and to be kind to others.'

Having a reason to spring into purposeful action each morning may be termed differently across the world. George referred to it as 'Way of Life'; I call it Focus on Why, but fundamentally, the essence remains the same. Crafting a purpose takes time and introspection. When you have clarity around why you want to achieve your intentions and your life priorities, decision making becomes significantly easier.

Understanding your true desires isn't always straightforward, and it's all too easy to postpone taking action. However, remember that it's your future self who ultimately suffers the consequences. Don't let this happen to you. Take yourself outside your comfort zone. Challenge the status quo. Growing, evolving and changing are all critical for living with purpose. Have the courage of your own convictions to break the mould. For me, my podcast has evolved into a lifelong project that brings immense joy. Serving as the curator of this remarkable living library, filled with stories of so many purpose-driven pioneers, is both a privilege and a source of pride.

George's Scrapbook
1 April 1940 – 19 June 1940

From waking up with the idea for my podcast on 1 April 2020, let's now rewind exactly 80 years to return to George's story. War is a stark reality. Knowing what he can and can't control, understanding the significant role he holds, his next step is to confront his reality – to grasp who he truly is and how he's living his life. Challenging the status quo, he evaluates the authenticity of his beliefs to ascertain if they match his values and contribute to his wellbeing.

> **1 April 1940, Le Havre**
> Now at last we are important. This is a land at war. This port is the conventional base of a land at war.

> **10 April 1940, Yvetôt, Seine-Inférieure**
> I saw again the platform where, 23 years ago, Daddy used to meet the ambulance trains.

Yvetôt in Normandy was a place of great personal significance as the Hôpital de l'Alliance was where his father, Dr James Rutherford Kerr CBE, CHM, was chief orthopaedic surgeon during World War One. Returning to a world he knows well as his family used to holiday here, George shares a moment of both familiarity and escapism.

> The countryside was peaceful and quiet now. Soissy and I strolled through the village streets as though we were walking in summer, in peacetime, as though, in a week, I should be back in school. Soissy took my arm and led me back to her little market square. She was very proud of her English officer.
> We talked to each other, Soissy in English, I in French. We discussed her drawings and my future – after the war. We played records of Jacques Trenet and Jean Sablon and she wanted me to write something in her autograph book. I could not think of

anything to write for her and so left it undone, promising to send it to her later.

As PMC I took some daffodils from the infants' school room next door, for the mess dining table. This is the first time I have attempted to sap the French war effort. They looked very lovely with the white cloth and cut glass.

12 April 1940, Le Havre

Reunion with Corvin Pearson. We dined well at the 'Gros Ton'. Later we went sightseeing in a brothel, Rue des Galions. Madame, Dickensian, monstrous and charming, sat outside in the evening sun, a huge greedy beetle.

Eventually I was left alone in the reception room with the remaining girls. I felt hideously priggish. I talked with Annette for an hour and a quarter. The least I could do was to buy innumerable bottles of acetic champagne. I told myself I was a Mass Observer, but I deceived nobody. Annette called me her 'petit Georges' and told me her story. She liked my naïveté and was, I suppose, quite glad of the rest. Madame was wheedling. She tried every way to get me to go upstairs, but I was adamant, and unbearably embarrassed.

George refers to the Mass-Observation project, which was a social research organisation founded in 1937. Essentially, its intention was to study the everyday lives of ordinary people in Britain. It is clear from all of George's work that he was a keen observer of people, but here he uses Mass Observer humorously in an effort to cover up his embarrassment.

At length we left, Madame and Annette both kissing me, Annette because she imagined I wanted to preserve some sense of superiority, Madame because she knew my cowardice and fear, and was laughing at it. Everybody acted very badly but the characterisation was good.

14 April 1940, Paris

My section and I crossed Paris luxuriously in a fleet of taxis. This, while unorthodox, is quite the best way of leading a section through Paris. Indeed it typifies at one and the same time both the quality of leadership in me, and adaptability in the British Tommie.

15 April 1940, Metz

We arrived at two o'clock on the morning of my 22nd birthday and formed up in the blue gloom of Metz station. I wondered whether to wear a tin hat. We listened for the sound of shells or planes. There was no sound.

16 April 1940

I went up to the British front line and beyond. A party of sappers blew up a stretch of road, four infantry officers played boats in a stream, and in the valley, ¾ mile away, I could see a church tower that was a German O.P. *[observation post]*.

Last night a German raiding party was shot up, and left some dead behind. This morning, staff cars, motorcycles and pedestrians had assembled as though for Jump Sunday at Aintree.

May 1940, Thionville

Supper with the Lax family at the Hotel Metropole; Madeleine, a very lovely girl. Jeannot, her brother, Luxembourgeois, fat, witty and cynical.

28 May 1940, La Ligne Maginot

Obligingly, the French shot up a section of German territory for us. There was no reply. Perhaps they didn't hear us. Perhaps they don't play at war in Germany.

10 June 1940

I helped to evacuate the Lax's belongings to Pont-à-Mousson, Meurthe et Moselle. Madeleine was machine-gunned on her way to church yesterday. I drove the 3-tonner by night through towns that had never seen an English soldier before.

June 1940, Woippy, Metz

Address to the troops at pay parade: 'I want to impress upon you the importance of this. The French are our allies. We must not offend or hurt them in any way. This is their livelihood. And if we damage it, not only may we impoverish the natives of Woippy, we may arouse feelings of distrust or dislike between the allies. You will remember therefore what Colonel le Grand has said and what I have said, that you are forbidden to steal strawberries from the fields, and that anyone found doing so will be severely punished.'

11 June 1940, Metz

At the Anglo-French dinner at the officers' club, we toasted 'L'Entente Cordiale', and murmured huskily to our neighbours 'd'accord'.

Paris fell to Nazi Germany on 14 June 1940. The mood shifts dramatically.

14 June 1940

The order came suddenly, and within 30 minutes the billets were empty and the men assembled at the sidings waiting for the train. All the hangars were empty and swept. The stores of food had been loaded two days ago and sent back to the base at Nantes. Debts that had accumulated since the outbreak of war had to be paid off hurriedly, and yesterday I walked the streets of Metz with over a million francs in my pocket.

At 11.45pm the train moved out of the sidings, and we left the hangars barren to the Germans. I had even troubled to remove the telephone, a Signal's fitting, and I carried it with me in the carriage. We rumbled over the Moselle, heading for Nantes and home. Through the dark we could see the tower of Metz Cathedral, and the glitter on the waters. On the wireless, a girl was singing to us from London. It was the late night dance music programme. Plaintively we wished we were a little nearer home.

15 June 1940

The English wireless is dead. Strasbourg spends its day telling the French dead:

' … Le Lieutenant André Morel, Nancy; Pierre de la Lune, soldat, Dijon; Alexandre de la Lune, soldat, Dijon; Philippe de la Lune, soldat, Chaumont; André Lamare, soldat, Épinal; Marcel Pierre, caporal, Mézières; le capitaine Charles Lemot, Belfort; Louis Lemot, soldat, Lyons…'

With George listening to a local radio station within range, this is an emotional entry recording those who'd perished, and bears a strong resemblance to the scene in Shakespeare's *Henry V*, where the long list of names of the French dead is recounted after the Battle of Agincourt.

16 June 1940

The German news tells us of the direction of the German advance. We are unable to turn West to make for Nantes because the Germans are at Verdun, Châlons-sur-Marne, Épernay, Bar-le-Duc. They are moving south, parallel with us, cutting us off.

We have decided to take the train due South through Nancy, Épinal, Vesoul, Lyons, and so to Marseilles. There it should be possible to get a boat to England or America. Meanwhile, our train does ten miles to the hour.

We ask for a driver and stoker from the men and get two volunteers. We threaten the French driver with a revolver, believing

49

him to be 'fifth column'. But the line is packed, sometimes for miles, with evacuee trains lying nose to tail.

We move forward at 30mph for a mile and a half, catch up on the chaotic convoy, and stop. Another jump of a mile, and a pause of 20 minutes. It becomes slower and slower, but if we leave the train here, we may miss one of the longer bursts of speed. We may lose 20 miles. And always we believe the line will clear.

We feel so impotent. We have to check an unreasonable but growing distaste for the civilians who are hindering us. But their motive is to run too, and we take stragglers on board. We are all so impotent.

Glorious weather! We sit in the sun, our feet dangling over the edge of the cattle truck. The train passes slowly through the Vosges. A sleepy village. We read the name of the tiny station. Charmes in the Vosges. How lovely!

I had never heard a bomb fall. The train had stopped and I was walking along the track. There was a German plane overhead, but it seemed harmless. I heard the smallest hint of a whistle of wind. No more. But all the literature of the last war combined to throw me flat in the ditch, seconds before the explosion came. Several more fell around the train. There was no damage.

A mile ahead of us, a plane is bombing the line. We fear a bridge is being destroyed, that our one line of communication has been cut. We may have to march. It is a long walk to Marseilles, but it is our only chance. We are ignorant now of the position of the Germans. We know nothing of the state of affairs in South France. Italy may have occupied Marseilles. The Germans may have gone through Switzerland.

Orders were given to abandon the train and the party split up: George and a group going one way; the rest head to the Swiss frontier. He shifts from 'I' to 'we' throughout the various entries to underscore the communal aspect of the shared journey, responsibility and challenges encountered. George feels a deep sense of responsibility for the party's safety and wellbeing, often emphasising their experiences rather than focusing solely on his own. His primary concern is food and shelter, demonstrating his unwavering commitment to fulfilling the immediate needs of his men.

17 June 1940, Rignosot, Doubs

We are very hungry after struggling through the woods and hills of the Bois Communes. We find a farm tucked away in the trees, and Madame and Mademoiselle cook eggs for the men, and give them glasses of milk. They refuse payment. I leave the money on the table in the kitchen. As we say goodbye, they wish us all 'Bonne chance', and then, from the goodness and the sadness of their hearts, they kiss me and cry.

18 June 1940, Deluz, Doubs

The Germans are close behind us. A tank has been seen; a parachutist has landed three miles back. We have walked for a day and a half and our rations are diminishing. Hitherto we have avoided villages and hurried over the main roads. But now we walk boldly, wearily down the main street of Deluz, and to the river bank. The River Doubs is a quarter of a mile wide and we are taken over by ferry. Crowds of villagers collect and tell us to hurry. 'The Germans are in the next village,' they say, 'you have no time to spare.'

Deluz is a lovely village. On the other bank of the Doubs, steep hills slope down to the water. The river winds round the valley, between green wooded slopes. We are tired, hungry and footsore. We have left our heavy kit in the train. I shall never see my Marvell again, or Bridges' 'Spirit of Man'. But we stuffed our pockets before leaving with cigarettes, emergency rations and biscuits.

We sit down behind a hedgerow at the water's edge. The sun is shining and we are brown and fit. But we are all dusty, tired. And here the villagers of Deluz bring us wine and chocolate and loaves of bread; and tell us to hurry. They lend us a guide to help us on our way; but we must hurry. 'A German is in the village now', they say,

> 'and buying provisions. Drink your wine, finish your bread and go.'
> It is the sweetest drink we have ever taken. We rise to our feet again.
> It has given us new life. Deluz has given us new life.

George stresses the exhaustion and hunger experienced by his group, again highlighting the urgency of meeting their core needs. Despite the pressing demands of their situation, he reflects on what holds personal significance: beauty in nature, lamenting the loss of his books, fortunate weather, their good health and the generosity of the villagers. Even when facing challenges and adversity, he found moments of consolation and connection, acknowledging the importance of human kindness and the small joys that bring him comfort.

> **19 June 1940**
> We should have slept all day as well as night. Last evening we had bought a lorry for 150 francs, and commandeered a second in the name of His Majesty's Government! We had set off in these for Marseilles, 700 miles away. But there were tanks ahead of us, and we had left the lorries after three miles. Then we had taken to the woods again, hidden ourselves and slept.
>
> I had intended to sleep through the next day too, and move only by night. We were obviously surrounded by German units. There had been heavy gunfire on the Swiss frontier that night, and all that long night too, lorries had rumbled past, and motorbikes and tanks. The men, however, wanted to get on. They didn't want to stay another night in those woods.
>
> Three hours later we were surrounded in a copse and fired on. Oliver was shot in the leg. We were without arms. I came out of the copse with my hands up.

As one challenge comes to an end, for George and these soldiers, this point marks the beginning of their next challenge.

Challenge: Reflections with Actions

↗ STATUS QUO REALITY CHECK

Take time to identify and question any assumptions, beliefs and values you've absorbed from familial, cultural or social influences over the years. Are they holding you back from reaching your full potential? Question any habits that may be detrimental to your wellbeing, identifying areas for improvement across all aspects of your life. This level of self-awareness will enable you to assess whether your current behaviours and choices align with your values and aspirations. By challenging ingrained beliefs and habits, you'll be paving the way for personal growth. Evaluate what changes you need to make and why they're important to you.

↗ KEY OBSERVATIONS

Reflecting on what you can and can't control, areas of responsibility and the choices and decisions available to you, what are your key observations from exploring these questions in depth?

Present: Who are you being? What are you doing? What do you have? What do you think about yourself now? What do others think of you? Where are you now versus where you want to be?

Future: Who do you want to be? What do you want to be doing? What do you want to have? What do you want to be thinking? What do you want others to be thinking of you?

Answering these questions will provide clarity on personal agency, acceptance of limitations, recognition of boundaries and your decision-making frameworks, ultimately empowering you to lead a more intentional and fulfilling life.

↗ OVERCOME CHALLENGES

Recall a past situation where you overcame a significant challenge. Reflect on the skills, strengths or resources you used to overcome it. Consider what you learned from the experience and how it influenced your growth. This will reveal valuable insights into your resilience, problem-solving and your capacity for adaptability, helping you navigate future challenges with confidence and determination. With wisdom gained from adversity and failure, you'll be able to turn future obstacles into opportunities for success.

Challenge: Celebrate and Continue

↗ Uniqueness

No one else in the world is like you – never has been, never will be. Your individual experiences, perspectives and qualities are what make you truly unique. Embrace your uniqueness. Reflect on what you've discovered about yourself through completing these exercises. Before continuing, acknowledge your journey of self-awareness and growth knowing that each insight is cause for celebration towards becoming the best version of yourself.

Step 2: Challenge – Summary

Your future self will thank you for the small steps forward you take each day. The accumulation of these small steps counts, as they compound over time, leading to significant progress. Remember, your present circumstances don't define you based on your past, nor do they determine your future indefinitely.

Step 3: Capture

Capture what matters: understand your needs, values, beliefs, aspirations, passions, gifts and strengths; know what you stand for and how you spend your time.

Now that you've taken control and challenged the status quo, the final step of **Part 1: Purpose** is to gain a deeper understanding of who you really are and how you want to serve others. To achieve this, capture and accurately document your core needs, values, beliefs, aspirations, passions, gifts and strengths.

Additionally, you'll need to have a clear understanding of how you spend your time, what's significant to you, what principles you stand for and how you intend to contribute to the wellbeing of others. These elements serve as the foundation for living with intentional purpose. By aligning your actions with your core values and aspirations, you can lead a life of meaning and significance, leaving behind a legacy that reflects your authentic self and contributes to the betterment of humanity.

Before building the life of purpose you desire, it's crucial to prioritise your core needs first. If you neglect your fundamental needs, life will quickly become very challenging, spiralling out of control, unable to help others. Begin by assessing how well you're addressing the core needs that serve as the foundation for your wellbeing: water intake, sleep quality, nutrition, time spent outdoors in nature, physical exercise, opportunities for leisure and enjoyment, social connection and emotional fulfilment.

Bombarded with conflicting advice and information from various sources, it's easy to feel overwhelmed by directives on diet, exercise and sleep patterns. However, recognising your individuality is key; what works for one person may not work for you, so prioritise discovering what combination best serves your mental, spiritual and physical wellbeing. To meet my core needs, I require eight hours of sleep nightly and a minimum of two litres of water (consumed by 9 pm to avoid sleep disruption). I aim for a minimum of two healthy meals daily with dinner eaten by 7 pm. I prioritise 30–60 minutes of outdoor walking daily and engage in 40 minutes of more intense exercise, four to five times a week. I value both solitude and social connection, balancing time alone with interactions with friends or family.

A word of warning. You may be aware of what you ought to do, but distinguishing between immediate desires and long-term intentions can be challenging. Despite understanding that what brings you comfort today might lead to discomfort later, you're often caught in this constant battle between instant versus deferred gratification. Every decision carries weight; your core needs are significant. Stay mindful of all your choices and their impact on the present day and weeks, months, years to come. Your actions today shape your future.

Next, let's focus on values. Values are abstract concepts, things you can't put in a shopping trolley, like autonomy, beauty, courage, freedom, justice, love and wisdom (although what a wonderful shop that would be). They define what you stand for and how you relate to the world through reflection and action. Mine are brilliance, connectedness, diversity, fun and growth. Eliciting values is one of the most powerful exercises I use with my coaching clients.

It's a process best done when facilitated by a coach, but one way to elicit your own values is by simply tuning into the news. Observe the stories, topics or issues that provoke strong emotional reactions. These core emotions and feelings provide valuable clues to the meanings behind what matters most to you. Pay attention to your reactions to instances of injustice. Reflect on what inspires you to effect change. Feelings such as frustration, concern, determination, discomfort, anger or sadness may signal that a value of integrity, justice, fairness, authenticity or compassion has been compromised.

Global challenges such as those identified in the UN Sustainable Development Goals may embody values such as solidarity, interconnectedness, environmental stewardship or human rights. News evoking inspiration, hope or joy could reveal underlying values of connection, love or freedom. By identifying your interests and concerns, you surface the core values that shape your beliefs, inform your opinions and motivate you to take action.

Values provide the framework for establishing personal boundaries, guiding what's acceptable and what's not across all areas of life. Living in alignment with your values creates fulfilment, liberation and inspiration, empowering you to spot more opportunities, to make wise decisions and informed choices. By creating meaningful, purposeful and innovative work that resonates with your values, you can tap into your potential more readily to achieve your aspirations. Align your work with your values to become valued for your work. In contrast, living in opposition to your core values can cause internal conflict or inconsistent outcomes. If you're exhausted, frustrated or overwhelmed and you find your work lacks fulfilment, it's probable that your endeavours are incongruent with your values.

Together with your purpose, your values serve as your inner compass, keeping you on track towards what holds genuine significance. Rather than adhering to perceived expectations, ensure that every choice and decision you make aligns with your values and desires. Remember you've already challenged your beliefs and their foundations, so remain authentic to yourself.

A key lesson in crafting a purposeful life is establishing a profound connection with yourself, then to recognise the connectedness you have with others. Prioritising self-care is essential, as it's your responsibility to tend to your own wellbeing before extending help to others. By practising self-care and self-love, you take a step closer to living a more fulfilled life with more capacity, inclination and energy to extend love to others.

Do you strive for perfection, self-criticise for unmet goals or perceive greener pastures elsewhere? Then know you're just one belief away from your greatest breakthrough or transformation. Achieving a healthier body, more wealth, business growth, improved relationships, or shifting from 'I'm not good enough' to 'I am good enough' is entirely within your grasp. It's your decision whether you reinforce a limiting belief or transform it into an empowering one. A limiting belief confines you by hindering your belief in having choices. Just one belief can be the difference between achieving your desires or facing obstacles.

After studying human behaviour for the last 30 years and facilitating more than 16,000 hypnosis sessions, Tim Shurr (FOW 127, 'One Belief Away') has discovered how to upgrade your unconscious mental programming so you can achieve and perform at the highest level. Tim said, 'I was surviving. I wasn't playing to win. I was playing not to lose. Stressed a lot. Always worried about money, always being broke. Always trying to figure out what my next move was going to be. And so I carried around a lot of pressure, a lot of insecurity, a lot of self-doubt.' Learning that his thoughts had influence over how he felt, that he was only ever 'one belief away' from changing them, Tim paid careful attention to what he was saying to himself.

Low self-worth can manifest in negative self-talk, leading to a lack of self-value or a belief of inadequacy, believing you're not good enough, preventing you from pursuing your dreams and creating the life you desire. By bringing awareness to your negative thoughts and choosing not to internalise them, you can overcome their influence. Thoughts are just thoughts; they're not reflective of reality. Valuing yourself and others, doing what brings you joy and remaining aligned with your values will guide you forward. Remember, how you feel is ultimately your choice.

Be mindful of using phrases such as 'I should', 'I need to' or 'I really must', as these might signify that you're adhering to others' values or priorities rather than your own. Instead, shift your language to 'I desire to', 'I choose to' or 'I love to' as these align more closely with your core values. Living and expressing your truth while showing self-compassion really makes a difference.

So, who are you? No, seriously, who are you really? Do you know? To help you answer, consider creating a Life Map, a visual timeline high-lighting key moments and experiences that have moulded who you are today. By completing your Life Map, not only will you recognise your accomplishments but also discern patterns and recurring themes that have consistently threaded their way through your life. You'll be able to identify connections between specific events and trends you've followed or consciously shaped over the years, all aligned with your core values.

Aged six, I used to play at being a librarian, pretending to stamp books, organising them into categories on my shelf. At 16, a careers' questionnaire suggested an ideal career for me would be a librarian. Friends had been offered other options such as lawyer, banker, vet, doctor or teacher. All I could picture was a bespectacled older lady working in dimly lit buildings surrounded by dusty books. Why would I possibly aspire to that?

How true that career prediction turned out to be though. All credit to the algorithms of that questionnaire, as now, decades later, I am that bespectacled librarian, surrounded by dusty books and proudly curating a library, albeit a global living library of purposeful people in the form of a podcast. Along with my inner librarian, my values, interests and passions had shown up very early in life.

When I initially completed this Life Map exercise, I arranged events chronologically, creating a horizontal representation resembling a heartbeat, with peaks and troughs reflecting the highs and lows of my life. The second time around, I wrote continuously for six pages, jotting down all the significant events as I recalled them without adhering to a timeline or editing the order of content. More recently, I mapped my life out onto an A1 sheet of paper, utilising colour coding to categorise different aspects, aiding in distinguishing all my entries to spot patterns.

Each time I've completed these visual Life Maps, not only have I been surprised by the extent of my achievements but clear patterns and themes emerge showing their alignment with my values. Drawn to hosting and facilitating events, I enjoy the role of collaborative leader standing alongside others rather than seeking the spotlight for myself – connectedness. A high level of commitment and focus, showcasing my ability to start and finish tasks effectively – brilliance. I'm proactive, often rolling up my sleeves to serve causes I believe in, and I prioritise fun. Understanding what fun looks like really helps incorporate more enjoyable activities into my daily routine.

Many of the threads converge under the theme of communication, with teaching, coaching, community-focused activities and the desire to effect change and transformation across various aspects of my life – growth and diversity. While I may not have labelled it as such, purpose has consistently guided my actions. This sentiment is best captured on my business card: 'Life is all about the people you meet and things you create with them. What we do together will shape the way we live in the future. A simple hello will lead to a million things.'

The Life Map also revealed my innate gifts, the strengths and passions I've developed. Gifts are your natural talents or abilities that come to you effortlessly, where in flow you lose all sense of time. Strengths are honed skills achieved over time after deliberate practice and dedication. Passions are specific activities, interests or pursuits you love engaging in most. Take time to recognise what your gifts, strengths and passions are and consider all the activities or tasks where you effortlessly excel as leveraging them is key to contributing positively to the world, bringing you a sense of fulfilment and living with purpose. How might your strengths, gifts and passions intersect with what the world needs?

Having played his role in WW2 as a navigator and bombardier, Don Clifton wanted to 'spend the rest of his life doing good for humankind'. To identify and explain the ways people most naturally think, feel and behave, he posed the great question, 'What if we studied what was right with people versus what's wrong with people?' The solution he provided was to create a profiling assessment tool now known as Gallup Clifton-Strengths, an option for you to consider in identifying your strengths.

The late Sir Ken Robinson, champion of the creative arts, challenged the effectiveness of schools and the way children are educated. His TED talk 'Do Schools Kill Creativity?' struck a chord with the inner child within every one of us whose freedom to explore innate curiosities was restricted. As there's a tendency for children to be encouraged to improve their weaker subjects at school instead of focusing on where they excel and develop innate gifts, strengths and passions, dreams are quashed, strengths inhibited and weaknesses highlighted. What a waste of talent, time and energy.

Remember how George helped me as a teenager enhance my performance with his reflections and recommended actions after attending my parents' evenings? He always focused on my gifts, strengths and passions. Now, working with my coaching clients, together we focus on these areas to explore opportunities and establish where best to invest talent, time and energy. So, comprehend your core values, needs and aspirations to capture your authentic self.

George's Scrapbook
20 June 1940 – 10 December 1940

Meanwhile, George wasn't concerned with capturing his authentic self.

20 June 1940, Besançon

We were captured at nine o'clock in the morning. At one o'clock on the next day we lay down wearily in the dew, in the arena of the stadium at Besançon. The Germans had marched us for 16 hours with brief rests every two hours. We have covered 58 kilometres. My feet were torn and blistered, and we were all weak with hunger.

After the war in July 1945, George reflected on this particular moment in an entry describing the experience in more detail.

We made several journeys across the German countryside in those five years, sometimes on foot, more often in sealed cattle-trucks, and through their ventilator slits we spied on the enemy land. We were curious to know whether life here was very different from life in the Lanarkshire orchards or on Shap Fells. Fundamentally, of course, it was the same. There were fewer cattle perhaps and no hedgerows, but great fields of alien corn waved in the wind.

We could see the peasants pause in their work, straightening their backs to watch our train rumble past. Sometimes, taking us for their own troops, they would wave to us. And we, as in Hampshire on our last journey before embarkation, and as in Normandy soon after landing, waved back.

We recorded in our minds, therefore, the Great Commonplaces of a people at war: soldiers cheered on their way, and peasants working in the fields. The stork by the water's edge, the Byzantine cupola of the Bavarian church, the empty chocolate machines on the country platforms, these only served to particularise this warring land as German. But for these, we might have believed the sleepy little station where our engine stood and puffed irritably to have been Adlestrop or Crome or Heathey Lane Halt.

At one such junction, we changed trains, and passing under the line by a subway passage came up on the other side to find a signpost pointing to left and to right. We took the left hand way which led to Laufen and to the first year of our captivity. That which pointed to the right, led to Berchtesgaden *[Adolf Hitler's Eagle's Nest was located here].*

22 June 1940, Besançon

I remembered my promise to Soissy and sent her a postcard for her autograph book.

Demonstrating friendship, honour and creativity, George fulfilled his promise to write a personal message in her autograph book as a keepsake. For Christmas 1977, George's gift to me was an autograph book filled with poems he'd written about me.

24 June 1940, Besançon

These maddening French! Whenever I walk in the prison yard, I am stopped and spoken to in villainous English. I walk on the dried mud and straw. I jostle my way through Senegalese, Poles, Belgians. Under the lime trees, the cavalry horses lie down to die. Occasionally, a German can be persuaded to destroy one; more often they are helped to life by the rations of their rider.

25 June 1940

'You mustn't let prison get you down, sonny. Once you do, you're finished.' Melodramatic fool! And this because I didn't shave this morning.

6 July 1940, The Black Forest

A charming girl of the Croix Rouge cycles up and down the line of prisoners with little gifts for them. She has evidently emptied a chemist's shop for us and we gladly, gratefully accept tablets and sweets and powders. Some we swallow, some we put on our feet.

I walk with four Poles. As an Englishman I attract the attention of the German guards. 'Eeenglish Tommy' they say, and laugh, and 'aus, aus!' they shout. For this reason the French are shy of me, but the Poles stay with me throughout. They are unbreakable.

Cars, lorries, tanks, tractors, motorbikes pour past us in the opposite direction, smothering us with dust. On their radiators French helmets are fixed, French swords sticking through them. Slogans in chalk cover the bodywork: 'On ne passe pas!', 'Jamais? Jamais? Jamais?' But everywhere the German troops behave well. They are the conquering heroes, and, jubilant, they laugh in our faces. But there is no looting, no drunkenness. Only lorry after lorry pouring the new culture into France, spreading it like a disease, over the face of Europe.

8 July 1940, Dulag XII, Mainz

In the Kantine one can buy a huge push ball for 2000 Reich Marks. I remember seeing it before the war in German Youth photos. In the yard, just outside my window, 17 French Generals are discussing the war!

Processed, then moved to Oflag VII C, Laufen, Bavaria on 11 July 1940, George described Laufen in his post-war entry from July 1945.

Laufen was a great solid building, humourless and grim. It had the character of a reform school, and one half expected to see pale faces at its hundred windows, or lines of children in striped blouses and thick wool stockings moving in weary crocodiles along its corridors or round and round its courtyards.

Laufen and Eichstätt both had the additional grace of running water passing within a stone's throw of the wire, both streams being sub-tributaries of the Danube; and at Laufen, the bridge spanning the Salzach led from Germany across into Austria. Further down the valley, we could see the wireless mast at Salzburg rising high over Mozart's birthplace. Laufen itself has music in its blood, for the organist in the church across the river had composed there the carol 'Stille Nacht, Heilige Nacht'.

We were fortunate in having those broad valleys to live in. We could follow for miles the peaceful course of the rivers, and the toy railway as it wandered past wooded slopes from village to village. At Warburg the trains were less intimate. They shrieked and raced past in a very business-like manner, intent evidently upon their arrival somewhere, while the Bavarian nursery engines might spend a lazy afternoon shunting back and forth along the local line.

11 July 1940, Oflag VII C, Laufen, Bavaria

'And now, gentlemen, you will be shaved. For naturally, in a camp like this we must be sure that you are clean.' These subtle insults! This was the final degradation, that we should be bronzed, fit – and bald!

Telegram dated 11 July 1940 to George's father and stepmother Amie

Regret to inform you that 2nd Lieut G F Kerr RASC is reported missing further particulars will be forwarded as soon as received. Under Secretary of State for War

Telegram dated 23 July 1940 to his father and Amie

Prisoner happy. George

July 1940

It was a terrible, sickly smell. I had walked in the same socks and boots for over a month. The socks I had been able to wash occasionally, but the sweat had infected the soles of the boots, and the fungus smelt strongly. I wondered whether it really was as powerful as I believed. I was embarrassed lest people should look at me and say 'unclean'. I had been so careful to stuff them beneath the bed. Could I still smell them? Yes, I could. I got out of bed and put them outside in the corridor.

September 1940
Two lectures were announced today. Metaphysics in the Garage and Applied Science in the Cobbler's Block. Because I was unable to buy in the Kantine either salt, razor blades, saccharine or cigarettes, I spent my money on Caesar's 'Gallic War'. It was either that or a scent spray! And then I found they had cut out the map of Gaul for security reasons!

Capturing the significance of his father's words he copied the letter into his scrapbook.

10 December 1940
Tonight I received the first letter from home since May dated 29 September 1940:

Dear George
Here likewise for our part, we worry only about you. So as these nearly balance we should be, as you say also, relatively happy. Be quite certain that the home fires will be burning all the time, the cloakroom door open (actually it always is, a custom I have fallen into, and persist in) and the dogs ready to shout their welcome.

In general, and in particular, and in fact we are all well, and work and routine go on as usual. Amie and I, and Rab and Boy *[George's dogs]* are very fit indeed. The garden is approaching its tints of autumn, leaves fall and keep Mr Primlett busy sweeping them up, and so on. Donald is very well and so is John, so all in all we have reason to be thankful. The Little Practice is thriving. We don't go out to anything – I haven't seen a film for nearly a year. I'll go when you return here – that's a good idea which I may be definitely held to.

As you say, things must be of better fundamental values in the future – for all nations – and so we hope for the speedy realisation of that by all the powers that be. I came across John's programme of the Berlin Olympic Games – what a pity that all that magnificent meeting couldn't have been continued always – in collaboration and friendship – instead of all being lost – pro tem. Well now – here's luck. Cheers and love from all of us, Daddy.

Letter received 12 February 1941 from Corporal Stan Davies
9 January 1941
Dear Mr Kerr

Hope you are well. 11 of the lads of your section are here with Hendy and myself, also a few of Section 7 (with Mr Gough, who has been ill for a long time) and some of the 'old brigade'. I had your address some time ago but cannot write often as we are restricted. However, the lads were all anxious that I should write to you (I am in the Office) so here it is at last.

We think of you a lot, and hope you are not too 'browned off', this isn't quite like the old 'jam session days'. You will be pleased to know Coates is with us too, and that Blakeley managed to make England. We lost a lot of the other lads but the ones that are here are ok. Hope you manage to get news from home. We do, often.

Do you need any books? We have lots. Please say. Anything you may need we shall get you if at all poss. Hope you had as good a Xmas as us. Section 9 toasted you all to themselves. If writing a letter here means robbing your people of one I shall understand. Boys all talk of Great Re-union after this is over, what about it? Unable to write a letter from this end yet, may alter later. Hopes.

Shall have to close. I will use the boys' own words. A good Officer and a Great Man. From Henderson. Cruddas. Coates. Perry. Brown. Green. Richards. Griffin. Parker. Oxley, and last but not least – Davies. Keep your chin up. Mr Gough often thought of you all. Cheerio, and a more fortunate 1941 than 40. Andrews and Gossy got through OK but not all.

Yours sincerely

Stan Davies

Cpl S Davies, British Military Internment Camp, Biezwil, Switzerland

Many were eager to learn of his circumstances yet with letters being restricted, they consolidated their enquiry illustrating that George mattered to them. 'A good Officer and a Great Man' elevated George's qualities and character above his soldiering abilities. Their touching offer to send books shows how well they knew him.

It's still early but already themes are emerging from George's entries and correspondence, especially the importance of bonds – between his family and friends, with other soldiers, among fellow POWs, between man and nature, and with the world of writers he connects with.

For George, as a POW, his identity and purpose had shifted; no longer needing to be the 'man in action', who would he be now? Who could he be? Would he attempt to escape? His scrapbook reflected this shift in thinking, dropping the documentation of daily happenings, with only two further entries for 1940. Instead he switched his attention to studying.

Capture: Reflections with Actions

↗ CORE NEEDS, FEELINGS AND VALUES

Understand what you need daily to function efficiently. Reflect on your core physical, emotional and psychological needs and consider how well they're currently being met in your life. Are you getting enough sleep, eating healthily, exercising regularly and practising gratitude? Make the necessary changes.

Complete the exercise I suggested by watching the news to elicit all the emotions triggered and the feelings they evoke, then answer this question – in the context of life, what's important to you? List out all the values that come up, and keep going until you have at least ten. Reorder them, prioritising their importance to you. Keep going until you are left with five you regard as being non-negotiable.

↗ LIFE MAP

Create your personal Life Map. Record significant milestones or events that have impacted you, along with any beliefs you've formed from them, obstacles encountered, challenges faced, failures, successes, best and worst decisions made, and risks taken. Allocate at least two to three hours to do this exercise in one sitting as it's a substantial undertaking. On completion, take time to reflect and observe emerging patterns and trends. What stands out for you?

Challenge your judgements, desires, aversions, motivations and impulses. Journal candidly about these aspects and question whether they truly align with your authentic self. Are your actions driven by genuine reasons? Identify any limiting beliefs, assumptions, fears or self-doubts holding you back from living a purposeful life. Challenge those beliefs by seeking evidence to the contrary or reframing them in a more empowering way. How can you shift your mindset to a growth-oriented perspective? Examine past events that prompted you to question your beliefs or act contrary to your values. These events provide valuable insights into the stance you take in the world. Reflect on how these events have been significant lessons in shaping your growth and influencing your current path.

🗡 Follow the Fun

Having fun triggers laughter and learning while releasing feel-good hormones like serotonin. In this pleasurable state, reduced levels of the stress hormone cortisol allow for increased focus and productivity. Embrace a playful mindset to invite more joy into your life.

Recall the enjoyable moments of your childhood: where were you, who were you with and what were you doing? Now, I'm not suggesting you start climbing trees again or chase your friends on your bike around the neighbourhood, although of course you can if that's what you desire. Instead look for patterns in the activities where you had the most fun as these memories hold clues to your sources of joy. Chances are similar preferences and activities will still bring you happiness today. Be more fun to have more fun!

Capture: Celebrate and Continue

🗡 Purposeful Moments

What makes you feel most alive, connected to your purpose or fulfilled? What brings you joy? How can you capture more of those experiences and incorporate them into your daily life? One effective method to nurture your overall wellbeing while staying aligned with your purpose is to capture the 'purposeful moments' that occur in your life: experiences, achievements, qualities, opportunities, strengths, testimonials, praise and compliments. Review your entries at the end of every week to identify patterns, themes or insights that emerge and notice how they align with your values. Remember to celebrate all your purposeful moments.

Step 3: Capture – Summary

In capturing your essence, not only do you gain insight into your true identity and motivations, you can develop your strategic plan with actionable steps. Without having this foundational self-awareness, you risk ambiguity around not knowing exactly what you want to pursue nor knowing which path to choose and create.

Part 1: Purpose – Summary

Through integrating these three steps, you've gained insights into what you can control, challenged your identity, enhanced self-awareness regarding your core needs, values, strengths, passions and gifts, and defined your aspirations and the stand you take. By consolidating this information, you'll be equipped to move to the next component. Before proceeding, revisit each of the three Reflections with Actions sections to ensure you've completed all the activities as they're carefully designed to help navigate uncertainties and clarify previously unknown aspects.

↗ Draft Your Purpose and Your Why

Now commit to writing your current understanding of your why and your purpose in just one line for each. Expect these concise statements to evolve as you progress through the next six steps. As a reminder, your purpose is the overarching intention that guides your direction in life. Your why is the emotional significance you assign to your purpose.

For inspiration, here are some examples:

Lauren Chiren (FOW 257, 'Women of a Certain Stage')
Why: Menopause misdiagnosed as early-onset dementia prompted a premature departure from a senior financial services role, igniting a mission to change the narrative on menstruation and menopause.
Purpose: Educate organisations globally to become menopause inclusive.

Jo Berry (FOW 223, 'The Gift of Conflict')
Why: Forgiving the IRA bomber for her father's death, transforming personal tragedy into global peacemaking.
Purpose: Encourage people to see humanity in others through conflict resolution.

Rob May (FOW 331, 'Educate and Entertain')
Why: Protect families and businesses from suffering consequences of cybersecurity attacks.
Purpose: Educate and entertain people with cybersecurity talks.

Isaac Kenyon (FOW 392, 'Healing Power of Nature')

Why: Crediting nature with saving his life after experiencing digital burnout.

Purpose: Create a positive impact through adventure connecting people, planet and wellbeing.

Charlotte Jones (FOW 351, 'From Fatigue to Freedom')

Why: Years battling chronic fatigue syndrome prompted comprehensive lifestyle reassessment in pursuit of full recovery.

Purpose: Promote global awareness on achieving freedom from fatigue.

Rikki Arundel (FOW 163, 'Dignity and Respect')

Why: Protect others from facing the same discrimination they experienced with their gender not being accepted and respected.

Purpose: Create a fairer world in which everyone has a voice and is heard.

PART 2
PLAN

Have a Plan
Step 4: Choose your actions
Step 5: Create and craft a plan
Step 6: Collaborate to amplify impact

In this part of the framework, you'll develop the plan needed to set intentions in alignment with your purpose and actively work towards achieving them. While it's important to have this plan, as life is full of obstacles, expect the possibility that it could be disrupted and you'll need to navigate challenges, setbacks and adversity. Rather than blocking your path, view these challenges as necessary parts of your journey revealing hidden opportunities.

Remember, your actions today shape your tomorrow, so remain open to change. In doing so, you'll continue to grow and expand beyond your comfort zone. Your plan needs to focus on your why so that you're naturally driven by intrinsic motivation, as your values shape and influence your actions. This will ensure you set values-based, purpose-driven intentions and milestones.

Remember that three-year plan I put in place back on 30 September 2016? It didn't need to be perfect; it just needed to hold personal emotional significance to get started.

Step 4: Choose

Choose your actions: your conscious choices and decisions will shape your meaningful, impactful legacy and channel your defined purpose.

German philosopher Friedrich Nietzsche said, 'The thought of a possibility can shake us and transform us.' (Ferrer 2021) Recognising that you have a choice in how you think, feel and behave is incredibly empowering. The quality of your choices determines the quality of your life and your purpose. Whatever you choose to conceive, believe or perceive will lead you to what's possible for you.

Discovering the root cause of larger issues and determining the necessary solutions could serve as the foundation of your purpose. Establish a courageous space for yourself to lead a life of purpose and responsibility to effect change and make a difference. South African Anglican bishop Desmond Tutu said, 'There comes a point where we need to stop just pulling people out of the river. We need to go upstream and find out why they're falling in.' (Bono 2021) Are you in the water waiting to be saved or are you striding with purpose along the bank to solve the problem? Change begins when individuals stand up for what they believe.

Purpose-driven people are trailblazing their own ways to solve problems in many different industries. Former lawyer Caroline Flanagan (FOW 380, 'Be the First') exemplifies how to become that trailblazer, showing what's possible and in doing so becoming an inspirational role model for her four sons. With her purpose to empower black lawyers to overcome barriers and bias and fulfil their potential to effect positive change, Caroline's call to action is 'Be the first'. This challenges them to understand they're not the only black person in a room; they're the first. This shift in thinking empowers them to act as pioneers, paving the way for others.

Caroline's powerful message of intentional self-perception can broadly apply to anyone rethinking their own potential and impact. Choice involves selecting the best or most appropriate course of action between available options. Every choice or decision you make determines the outcome. You weren't born with your habits or beliefs; they're chosen, adopted and reinforced. Your choices shape your actions, and when practised over time they become your habits, but you have the power to change your life by changing your choices. Are you in the water or are you on the bank? This is the choice you get to make.

In the compilation episode FOW 300 'Strength of Purpose', Mandy Hickson described her relentless pursuit of an impossible dream despite numerous setbacks to become the second woman to fly a Tornado GR4 on the front line for the RAF. Recognising her responsibility to inspire future generations, in FOW 301, 'Just Like You', Mandy reflected on an encounter with a young cadet that ignited her overarching purpose, guiding her transition into a second career as keynote speaker, where she continues to illuminate the path for others.

In the challenging year of 2020, plagued by restrictions, lockdowns and setbacks for many, I seized the opportunity to pause and reset. Instead of succumbing to the difficulties, I thrived and excelled, experiencing personal and professional growth. It brings me immense joy to know that through the wonderful *Focus on WHY* podcast platform, I've been able to help others reveal meaning and purpose in their lives. By aligning with my values, and while fulfilling my purpose, I'm also proud to be creating a living legacy.

Your legacy is far more than being what you amass in terms of an estate; it's about the lasting impact, influence and inspiration you leave behind. Legacy isn't just about what happens after you die, either; it's about what you accomplish and the contributions you make while you're alive. Without consciously choosing to leave a legacy, you may lack a sense of purpose or meaning in life.

Many of my podcast guests speak of a living legacy being a critical part of their purpose. In FOW 132, 'Becoming More Significant', Sylvia Baldock explained that her work is focused on significance: 'It's not about the material things in life; it's about the difference you make on this planet. It's about the lasting impact you have on the people you share your life with. You're living your legacy right now.'

Every one of us has the power to effect change. Each day lived with purpose contributes to your legacy. Your future is influenced by how you spend each moment of each day punctuating it with the significance that every moment matters. Regularly block out time in your diary to focus on your purpose. Take the opportunity to pause in your busy daily life to re-evaluate whether you've drifted off course.

Reflecting on how my grandparents influenced, impacted and inspired me to live with purpose, I deeply appreciate the time they spent with me and all the precious memories we created and shared. Their legacy lives on through this collaborative book. Understanding how I might be remembered and knowing I've made a difference gives my life profound meaning and helps me become reconciled to my own mortality.

While walking the dog and dodging the April showers, Holly and I noticed how the overnight frost had struck the magnificent magnolias in full bloom. Taking a shortcut across the common through the banks of beautiful daffodils, Holly pointed out that we were on a 'desire path' and explained how they're routes created by people or animals through repeated use, often seen as more direct than designated paths; unofficial desire paths become more defined and visible over time.

Similarly, this analogy can describe the way we form new neural pathways. The more you practise a habit, the more ingrained it becomes in your brain, eventually becoming your natural way of behaving or thinking. What about your metaphorical desire path? Just like a physical desire path, when you know where you're heading, you can choose how and where to carve this path to get to exactly where you want to travel. Knowing that you're working towards something you're passionate about, aligned with the stand you take, gives you a reason to jump out of bed each day. In the pursuit of achieving these purposeful and meaningful intentions, it's the journey that brings fulfilment.

Walking this type of path of desire requires determination, persistence and focus. You need clarity of vision to create a plan, set specific intentions and milestones, take daily action and be flexible enough to adjust along the way. You may need to develop new skills, pick yourself back up having learned from your failures, and push yourself out of your comfort zone to achieve your intentions.

To create this book, I needed the support of a coach to help me believe in myself and my writing ability. In that coaching session, I surfaced the limiting belief that 'I didn't think I was good enough to write a book on the subject of purpose'. Encouraged in the session to create a new belief, I chose to believe that 'I am a powerful writer who has the ability to change people's lives with my words'. As I spoke those words out loud, I realised I'd already been helping people change their lives for years, creating positive, global ripple effects through my coaching, podcasting and blog writing.

I'd revered George for his endless creativity, writing plays for stage, TV and radio, as well as novels and short stories, but I'd totally dismissed and not acknowledged all the work I'd been creating because it was in different formats addressing different audiences. The block that prevented me from being creative magically disappeared, and I wrote this book. So, if you're thinking 'Maybe one day, I'll…', then now's the time to act.

When you follow your desires, you'll likely also face false starts, setbacks, doubts or fears, all hindering your progress. To maintain your focus on purpose and develop a well-crafted plan, it's essential to have a deep understanding of what truly matters to you. By reframing challenges as necessary components of your journey and opportunities for growth, you'll remain committed to your purpose, even in the face of adversity. This shift in mindset empowers you to stay on course and maintain focus on the greater intentions. Define your purpose, practise mindfulness and welcome obstacles as opportunities to focus and shape your purpose-driven plan. To overcome any fears to achieve what you desire, I advocate what Stoic philosopher Seneca described as *euthymia*, 'Believing in yourself and trusting you are on the right path, and not being in doubt by following the myriad of footpaths of those wandering in every direction.' (Holiday and Hanselman 2016)

Also advocating the concept of *eudaimonia* (flourishing in the pursuit of what's worthwhile in life, which is essential to thriving), Greek philosopher Aristotle believed that 'happiness is the meaning and purpose of life, the whole aim and end of human existence' (Dobrin 2013). When you combine eudaimonia with the emotional stability provided by euthymia, it essentially means you have the clarity to choose the purposeful desire path, trusting and believing it's the right one for you to flourish in its pursuit. Identifying, pursuing and staying on an authentic path aligned with your values means you're less likely to experience regret or feel you're living someone else's life. Is your desire path one crafted from both euthymia and eudaimonia?

What cause or issue do you feel compelled to champion or help solve? Whatever you choose, know it triggers a ripple effect: as you serve, you grow; as you grow, you serve. Consider how your acts of service might create a positive impact and contribute to making the world a better place. It's your responsibility to shape the future landscape of our planet. Be mindful, ethical and responsible in your actions as an individual as they all compound and collectively make a significant difference.

George's Scrapbook
15 February 1941 – September 1941

George has been moved again, from Oflag VII C/H Laufen to Oflag VII D in Tittmoning. In a later entry taken from July 1945, he describes Tittmoning.

The schloss at Tittmoning had been a Youth Hostel before the war, a lovely place to come to at the end of a day's walk, provided one approached it from the North, for it was perched high on a rocky hill, and the climb up from the village must surely have discouraged all but the most youthful. It discouraged us when first we came there, but the threat of a bullet if we dropped out of the line put spirit in us.

The courtyard of the schloss looked like the stage set for some village idyll. There was a moat girdling the place where ducks paddled beneath the wooden footbridge. An arched gateway led into the court within, and here in this mock-village square there was a row of tiny cottages, a church front, dark, vaulted cellars and twisting outside stairs, a fountain and a drinking trough, window boxes and ivy on the walls, a lime tree, a blackbird in its branches, and – surrounding the whole miniature village, and acting as our camp boundary – the gabled, turreted walls of the schloss itself.

15 February 1941, Tittmoning, Bavaria
From a YMCA essay on 'New Thoughts of a Prisoner occasioned by his imprisonment'
But even now we are mentally inert, like the humanity of T S Eliot 'living, and partly living'. A seclusion more complete than prison. Nowhere have there been fewer distractions. And time, the plaint of us all once, now appears to us in its reality, immeasurable, infinite.

George has taken responsibility for his own thoughts and circumstances, so that even in prison and experiencing hardship, he remains free to reflect. The phrase from T S Eliot, 'living and partly living' (from

Murder in the Cathedral), is very much like the difference between living and existing I highlighted earlier.

> There is so much work to be done; there are so many urgent problems to be solved.
>
> We can guess too, at the latent beauty of thought in each of us, the inherent nobility of gesture. All this is for us to develop in ourselves, but to a large extent we make our own conditions.
>
> Perhaps I am beginning to concentrate again. Quiet here, too, if we listen hard enough for it, quiet if only in contemplation, in memory, in reflection…

In *A Month of Sundays,* George speaks of the life cycles POWs experience. New Kriegies spent early days mapping, the rest of their first year learning a language or sentimentally listening to Tchaikovsky. The second year was spent reading *War and Peace* and painting watercolours. Then depression and religious melancholia set in.

While I was at university, after I'd been enthusing about a concert at the Royal Festival Hall, George wrote to me demonstrating how he'd practised Reflection with Action as a POW.

> ***Extract from a letter dated 10 November 1993 to me from George***
> We're delighted you've met Tchaikovsky. It is extraordinary how he always opens the door. He did for me in prison camp. I suppose because we are first and foremost Romantic – as, of course, he is. In prison we had a Gramophone Society, met once a fortnight and played different records, then talked about them.

> **April 1941**
> I know, of course, that someone must play Icarus to John's Daedalus, the cunning craftsman. I know too that to Donald it will be the only life and that he will be better fitted for it than most. I am being selfish. I'm afraid and I'm sorry he is doing it only because he will do it so well. The man of action is outside my understanding and

> flying is another world to me. But tell him to be careful and to look after himself.

This is an extract from a letter he'd sent to his father, which he'd written in his scrapbook. He's concerned for his brothers' lives, particularly Donald's. George, feeling inadequate as a soldier compared to his brothers, shares his shortcomings. Lacking courage, he admired their choices: Donald following what he desired and excelled at, despite the risks, and John pursuing medicine as his 'Way of Life'.

August 1941
Macmurray's 'Freedom in the Modern World' diagnoses and prescribes for some of my 'immortal longings'. But my reading is always bad, nervous and careless, and I adapt thoughtlessly. Hence the 'magic' perhaps in a voice of reason!

Through the questioning of his own mortality, you can sense George's pain as he wrangles with the meaning of his existence. Reading Macmurray's book brought some solace as he recognised he was not alone in his existential questioning. As a man of reason, George managed to retain his sanity in prison through his choice of extensive reading, studying and writing.

August 1941
The speaking of Shakespeare's words in public gives a very full sense of pleasure. One glories in the victory Shakespeare has had; one is drawn with the words almost level with him. One smiles in sympathy with those poor mortals, the audience, with the actors, with oneself. But there is this unconscious effort too to help the world to an understanding of what is being said and felt.

Packed houses for 'Hamlet', requests for extra performances. The whole production is a triumph for Michael's honesty, simplicity and talent.

From the reading room window one can see all the plain laid

out beneath the evening mist which drags from the river, curling lazily. There is an interval in the play, and the lute and recorder are playing 'Greensleeves'. The sadness of a vanished period and the exultation of the present unite to make us remember the World War and its relative position. Is it important? Is 'Hamlet' important? Are we escaping from something here? Or are those who are fighting escaping? How remote the war is! And how remote this dialogue of Reynaldo and the old fool Polonius that we can hear as we gaze out into the summer night.

The POWs demonstrated their resourcefulness by wearing costumes and wigs from the Munich Opera House and make-up from Berlin, with local resident photographer Dr Jung capturing the production. Through these performances, escaping from the hideous reality of war, they entertained and inspired an audience while exploring themes of identity, friendship, politics, family, mortality, revenge and the consequences of action versus inaction.

In this production George played Horatio – a character known for his discernment, intelligence and unwavering loyalty as a trusted friend and confidant to Hamlet, played by Michael Goodliffe. As the survivor who gets to tell the story, how fitting a role for George. I wonder also if this moment is why he held such a treasured, lifelong connection with Shakespeare, even prompting our entire family's relocation to Stratford-upon-Avon. In George's darkest moments during imprisonment, poetry and literature provided an escape from reality and served as a cathartic release for a range of emotions.

September 1941

The five days' wonder was completed. I felt flushed and triumphant, not at the quality of the play itself, but at this leaping of the first obstacle. How many times in the last three years had I started to write a play? How many titles had I written at the head of my paper? 'Porfidy's Peace', 'And deeper greens', 'Mirrored Fantasy', 'Tortured Poppies', there were so many. And now at last I had written a full

> length play! 'Land that I heard of', a play in three acts by George Fleming Kerr.
>
> It is an attempt to summarise and set down myself and my family during the years of my maturity. I have come, in time if in nothing more, so far, and I wanted to show myself how far I had come and by what route.

During the endless hours of confinement, he fulfilled a long-held desire by completing his first play, *Land that I heard of*. The significance lay not in its quality but in its completion. Through documenting his journey, he'd witnessed his own growth and progress over time, reinforcing the importance of regularly journaling. He'd captured his creativity and been inspired by the song line from *The Wizard of Oz* he'd documented on 27 March 1940.

> **September 1941**
>
> As I went upstairs to the Ridderzaal, David Ross passed me. He was in a pale blue pullover, his cheeks were pink and his eyes very blue. He smiled as we passed. The moment had lent him much of the glory of this summer's evening.
>
> As I wrote, upstairs in the Ridderzaal, I knew David Ross was cutting the wire and crawling through. As the shots sounded, my heart sank. I couldn't write. I couldn't move from my table. I could only repeat over and over again to myself, 'These damnable old men. These damnable old men.'
>
> As he was marched across the yard to the gaol, he passed Clough, the German Adjutant. Ross was in Bavarian costume and, as he passed, he raised his arm in the Nazi salute. It was an impromptu, brilliant gesture. He felt the part he was playing and he played it well.
>
> This evening Clough, whom we all respected as a Prussian and a gentleman, lost his control. He was so angry. The English laughed at his fallen greatness. And all the attributes of tragedy were in this evening.

As George shared in the 1990 interview, he'd viewed attempting to escape through the wire 'extremely perilous'. For him, the only escape possible was through his mind.

In October 1941, George was transferred to Warburg until 12 September 1942, and he described the camp in his post-war entry from July 1945.

Warburg was a prison camp; it had pretensions to nothing else. The conception was simple and inelegant, based on the theme of the English holiday camp. The unit was a hut, long, low and with a structure of wood or concrete, and these huts were settled formlessly about the bleak compound.

The simplicity of the system was that as more prisoners were taken, more units could be built. By the time we reached Warburg, however, we had come to expect so little of the Germans that we were agreeably surprised to learn that the huts in which we were searched were not to be our homes, but were considered indeed as 'unfinished'. They lacked windows and floorboards, and the walls were very, very damp but, wondering at our luck, we were led to our true homes. It must be remembered, though, how much time improved the appearance of the camp; thousands of little windows twinkled through the ground mist.

Unlike the three camps in Bavaria, within walking distance of the Austrian Tirol, in Westphalia there were no hills to limit the view, and the Warburg plain had the appearance of a Dutch landscape, its monotony of space and atmosphere broken by a spindly tree or a plough on the skyline, by clouds whipped into angry shapes by a cruel wind, or by the spire and roofs of Dössel-bei-Warburg, all we could see of this mysterious village, so closely did it nestle to the earth, out of the gale.

Choose: Reflections with Actions

✈ Desire Path

What's your vision for tomorrow? Choice opens up possibilities! To create and design your own desire path, begin by envisioning it as if you've already traversed it to the fullest, reaching the end of a life rich in fulfilment and purpose. Now reflect on all your wonderful years, the actions taken, the emotions felt along the journey. What happened? Where did your desire path lead you? What did you see? What was your purpose? What living legacy did you create? What qualities and values define your life's work? Journal all the details of the desire path you carved.

✈ Mindfulness Meditation

By practising mindfulness, you anchor yourself in the present moment and avoid being overwhelmed by past regrets or future anxieties. Spend a few moments each day by yourself in a quiet space. Close your eyes and focus on your breath, noticing each inhale and exhale. Bring awareness to your body, scan it from head to toe, releasing any tension or discomfort. Observe your thoughts and emotions without judgement. Acknowledge them but don't allow them to control you. Mindfulness improves with practice and will help create a calmer, more centred 'Way of Life'.

✈ Now's the Time!

If you've been thinking, 'Maybe one day, I'll… [fill in here whatever you desire to achieve in life]' then now's the time to act. Now's the time to… write that book, take up that new hobby, reinvent yourself, switch careers, start a business, create a more purposeful life. Make a list of all the things you've ever wanted to do, then take action and get living. Switch this from a To Do list into a To Be list.

Choose: Celebrate and Continue

➤ EUTHYMIA AND EUDAIMONIA

At the end of each day, identify and celebrate all the choices you faced and decisions you made that were based on self-trust and courage of conviction. In doing so, you acknowledge you're walking your own desire path and flourishing in its pursuit.

Step 4: Choose – Summary

Take control of your destiny and carve your own path. Your thoughts influence your actions to shape who you become and what you achieve. What you do and what you have are within your control. By making deliberate choices, you pave the way for opportunities to align with your purpose and leave a lasting legacy that can resonate through generations to come. Are you living or merely existing? You choose.

Step 5: Create

Create and craft a plan: expand your creativity, thinking and network with intention, meaning and joy to create new possibilities and opportunities.

Viktor Frankl's theory of logotherapy was founded on combining the broader meaning of human existence with the individual's search for personal meaning in life. This 'striving to find a meaning' Frankl referred to as 'will to meaning' and considered it to be the 'primary motivational force' of human existence. He believed that 'life never ceases to hold a meaning' and proposed that meaning can be found in one of three directions (Frankl 1969).

The first direction refers to what you give to the world. In terms of your creations, this can be actioned from within any area of life and might include professional accomplishments, creating art, music or literature or other creative pursuits, religion or philosophy, acts of service, charitable work for a cause or organisation, volunteering work in the community, personal development, hobbies or interests, helping family and friends in need, mentoring or coaching.

The second direction refers to what you gain or take from the world, either through your experiences or encounters, or from loving another person. Examples could come from experiencing beauty found in nature, art, music, culture or experiencing love as it lifts your spirits and stirs your soul to create wonderful memories.

The third direction refers to the stand you take in response to a predicament. From a struggle, pain or unavoidable suffering emerges a meaningful, emotional why, acting as a powerful catalyst for purposeful work. From what I've observed occurring in interviews on my podcast, the loss of loved ones, near-death experiences or adversity have all prompted deep reflection, a reassessment of priorities and clarification of values eventually leading to healthier life choices and habits, the pursuit of personal growth, empathy for others, dedication to service and a desire to leave a lasting legacy.

However, I need to stress that finding meaning in life doesn't require personal suffering. The purpose of life is to *live* with purpose, creating it through your actions and building meaning into your life through reflection. When you notice what it is you gain and how you respond to all circumstances, you'll recognise that meaning is present in every moment and simply requires you to take action. But what action will that be?

Creative business legacy strategist Julie Creffield (FOW 137 'Chasing Freedom'), explained that there is 'opportunity everywhere especially when faced with real adversity, the creative side of us comes out. We create something that wasn't even an idea before. It comes out of nowhere. With confidence, pursue what interests you, be yourself, even if that means you're different from everybody else, show up unapologetically as you are. Trust the right people will find you.'

Consider the barriers preventing you from living with purpose. Are they rooted in fear, self-sabotage, doubt or insecurity? Do you perceive yourself as too old or too young? Perhaps you believe you lack time, money or effort. Whatever it is that's preventing you from taking action, take a moment to appreciate the possibilities awaiting you if you liberate yourself from these constraints and limitations. What destinations do you aspire to reach? What creations do you wish to bring to life?

You hold the responsibility to create the life you want to live. You have the power to make it happen. Understand that your purpose is bigger than all fears, doubts and insecurities combined. Limited only by yourself, once you set your creativity free, the possibilities become limitless. Wake up your inner genius and expand your thinking through creative living. Learning how to interpret the significance of life experiences and encounters will help you facilitate a purposeful 'Way of Life'.

You may not think so or even choose to call yourself one, but you're a creator in your own unique way, and every day you're creating your life path. Looking at your life from an external perspective, you'd see the endless choices of different paths you disregard as you opt for a favoured route. Decisions and choices that you make each day make a difference over time. You're responsible for creating your life of purpose. For example, do you take your health for granted? If you don't take care of your body today, how will you live tomorrow? A sobering thought! How about if you were told the date you were going to die – would you be doing what you're doing right now?

Creating a life of meaning and purpose is unique to you, which is why I've asked you to understand what you can and can't control, challenge the status quo, capture who you really are and choose what's important to you. With self-reflection and self-awareness, choosing and focusing on what truly matters to you, what brings you joy and what you excel at, you have everything you need to create the authentic life you really want.

Encouraged to read from a young age, my life has been greatly influenced by books, particularly in creating my purposeful journey. One such book is *Ikigai* (2016) by Héctor García and Francesc Miralles. When I interviewed author Héctor García (FOW 39, 'Create Your Ikigai'), he said, 'You have to believe that there is one ikigai [your reason for being] or there can be many ikigais for you. You are responsible for finding or creating it. You have to never give up because every human being is made, built for purpose, driven by purpose. The main core message is that we need to have that purpose. It's the most important thing.'

Purpose and meaning permeate every aspect of your life, whether you're aware of it or not. The distinctive patterns and themes identified in the Life Map exercise (in the Choose step) serve as the golden threads necessary for you to create and craft your life of purpose. These golden threads reveal your identity, aspirations and destinations. Your experiences are uniquely yours. No one else has walked the same path as you. Trust in your ability as a creator, and with creativity, confidence and courage, pursue your passions with your purpose and a plan.

In FOW 239, 'Play a Much Bigger Game', business coach and mastermind mentor Paul Avins explained how having suffered a near-death experience changed his life forever. Paul now sees his gift as helping businesses solve their issues of time and money to enable them to 'open up their creativity and play a much bigger game, have a much bigger impact on the world and ultimately contribute far more value to the world'.

Remaining positively curious enhances your problem-solving and creativity. What will you choose to explore with curiosity today? Don't let fear of judgement or criticism hinder your questioning. You can't control what others think so be inquisitive and ask questions. People love answering questions, sharing their knowledge and insights, and as well as building and strengthening better connections with them, you'll likely increase your capacity for openness to learning and growth.

Let your curiosity flow and lead the way. Challenge your thinking patterns by shifting your language and your mindset. Instead of thinking in terms of limitations, saying 'I can't do that because...' or 'That's not possible...', shift your language to focus on possibilities. Adopt a positive, 'How can I?' attitude prompting your brain to search for solutions to your challenges. Additionally, place the magical word 'yet' at the end of your statements to instantly transform impossibility into possibility and negativity into positivity. 'I don't know how...' becomes 'I don't know how... yet' or 'I'm not...' becomes 'I'm not... yet'.

Be curious. Embrace learning. Develop your ideas, hone them and take focused action to bring them to fruition. An idea without a plan stays just that – an idea. As my Focus on Why Framework illustrates, purpose is fluid, evolving alongside you, adapting to your changing circumstances. As you transition through different stages of life, your priorities and purpose will naturally evolve together. What positive beliefs do you uphold, and how do you approach learning? What 'Way of Life' are you carving? What new doors are you going to open? The future belongs to those who are curious. It's never too late to be who you might have been!

Facing grief, anxiety, menopause and a knee injury, Jo Moseley (FOW 295, 'Calm Confidence') recovered and reclaimed her identity by taking to the water. The first woman to paddleboard coast to coast in the UK, not only did she clean the waterways and fundraise along the way, she gained movement, freedom and calm confidence. In creating a more purposeful 'Way of Life', Jo's exploration as a joy encourager, midlife adventurer and beach cleaner also led her to becoming a bestselling author of two paddleboarding books.

In the initial 40 years of life, you're busy navigating numerous transitions that emerge, encompassing education, career advancement, personal relationships, marriage and parenthood. However, in contrast to your first 40 years, in midlife there's a significant shift of emphasis on inner reflection, involving a comprehensive review of various aspects such as career, business, finances, relationships, personal development, health and contribution to society. Priorities in midlife now gravitate towards focusing on purpose, legacy and contribution. This existential questioning is often what prompts the need to suddenly 'find' your why.

Are you feeling aligned with the mission and purpose of your work? Do you sense fulfilment and understand how your role fits in the bigger jigsaw of life? Are you making a meaningful difference? If not, I'm not suggesting an immediate career change. Instead, first consider ways to align your strengths, values and personal mission with the values, mission, vision and purpose of your current company. Many of my coaching clients have proposed minor adjustments to their job descriptions, roles and responsibilities to gain enhanced joy and fulfilment within their existing positions. What changes could you implement to ensure your current role is more purposeful and fulfilling?

A change in your current role isn't the sole pathway to a purposeful life. Any role focused on purpose or centred on service where you can align your values with those of others, share a vision and take responsibility for your contribution to the world can lead to a more purposeful life. This might involve becoming an entrepreneur, taking on a voluntary role in your community or perhaps creating your purpose around enjoyment, leisure and adventure. Your options are infinite.

Have your children flown and grown leaving you with an empty nest and now you're contemplating how your identity and purpose will evolve through this transition? Do you find yourself sandwiched between generations, balancing the needs of ageing parents with the responsibilities of supporting children transitioning into early adulthood? Despite these demands of caregiving and planning for the future, recognise the importance of embracing each day as an opportunity for growth and fulfilment. Awareness of mortality becomes increasingly palpable, especially if, as I have, you've experienced the loss of friends and family members.

From the end of midlife to your final years, retirement beckons in whatever form that may take, bringing with it a new phase of purpose and meaning. This transition prompts another shift into what truly matters to you now – your contribution to the world and the legacy you'll leave behind. However, there's no need to wait until this point to embrace this perspective. By clarifying your purpose now, you can align your actions with your mission and your vision, seizing each day as an opportunity to make an impact.

Despite the uniqueness of each individual's story, everyone possesses a distinct purpose and why that drives them forward. Listen to the podcast *Focus on WHY* to witness how purposeful actions create positive global ripple effects, showcasing how purpose transcends individuality to gain greater significance. This is how your purpose becomes bigger than you, emphasising the importance of every moment and the impact of your actions on shaping the future.

George's Scrapbook
November 1941 – 14 July 1942

November 1941

I didn't notice at first, but now, on looking through the letters of the last month or so, news of Donald is either slight or vague: 'We haven't heard from Donald lately' or 'John is very fit and well'. And now a letter which speaks of him as though he were, in fact, missing: 'We have not heard from Donald for some time, but no news may be good news.'

Months ago I regretted my stupid reference to Icarus. I withdrew all I had said, and prayed that Donald had not been told of my regret that he should take to wings. What a hopeless discouragement it must have been.

George's family had known Donald had been missing in action for several months but hadn't relayed their concern nor shared they'd received a telegram from the under-secretary of state, Air Ministry, reporting Donald missing as a result of air operations on 4 June 1941. Or if they had, it had either not been delivered or had been censored as George didn't know of his brother's fate.

Marcus Aurelius

'Men seek out retreats for themselves, cottages in the country, lovely seashores and mountains. Thou too art disposed to hanker greatly after such things; and yet all this is the very commonest stupidity; for it is in thy power, whenever thou wilt, to retire into thyself: and nowhere is there any place whereto a man may retire quieter and more free from politics than his own soul; above all if he have within him thoughts such as he need only regard attentively to be at perfect ease: and that ease is nothing else than a well-ordered mind.

Constantly then use this retreat, and renew thyself therein: and be thy principles brief and elementary, which, as soon as ever thou recur to them, will suffice to wash thy soul entirely clean, and send thee back without vexation to whatso'er awaiteth thee.'

This excerpt from the Roman emperor and Stoic philosopher Marcus Aurelius would alone have been sufficient enough to navigate a life of captivity. Realising he possessed the freedom of his own mind, George could turn inward to retreat at any moment to explore his own thoughts and embark on metaphysical walks. Self-reflection became his sanctuary, an inner haven impenetrable by anyone. In the midst of war, his mind and imagination provided a sense of peace. Ironically, this passage also planted a seed for a future quest to find solace in a 'cottage in the country' for himself.

I can appreciate how Marcus Aurelius's *Meditations* would have provided George with the wisdom and practical guidance necessary for a meaningful life, instilling in him the courage and resilience needed to endure those unknown POW years. Patience became one of George's strengths, a virtue Marcus Aurelius himself cultivated during his own wartime campaign in central Europe many centuries ago, coincidentally not far from where George was being held captive.

Plato's *Symposium*

'This life, my dear Socrates, said Diotima, if any life at all is worth living, is the life that a man should live, in the contemplation of absolute Beauty. And are you not rather convinced that he who thus sees Beauty as only it can be seen, will be specially fortuned? And that, since he is in contact not with images but with realities, he will give birth not to images, but to very Truth itself? And being thus the parent and nurse of true virtue it will be his lot to become a friend of God, and, so far as any man can be, immortal and absolute.'

Beauty flourishes in the realm of human connection. The true essence of beauty emerges through meaningful relationships marked by love, kindness and compassion. By uplifting and supporting others, you create a ripple effect that magnifies the beauty within yourself and all those around you. Pause to appreciate how impactful and meaningful experiencing beauty is in your life, how it touches you, because then you'll understand how essential it is to creating and living a purposeful life.

Keats' Letters
'There is an awful warmth about my heart like a load of immortality.'
'I am certain of nothing but of the holiness of that heart's affections, and the truth of Imagination. What the Imagination says as Beauty must be truth…'

Keats speaks of insights into reality from imagination, dreams and creativity. George knows he must remain true to his soul and pursue his own truth through perception, imagination and beauty in life. By contemplating the transient nature of life and the inevitability of death, it serves as a reminder to align your actions and intentions with what's meaningful and lasting.

January 1942
A letter comes from the Russian prisoners:
' …now the winter is coming and we are all beginning to die. We ask you to help us and we know that our request will not be forgotten. We ask for your help only because without it we cannot live.'

Heartbroken and powerless, George could only document their plea.

1 February 1942
'As I told you, in letters which you apparently didn't receive, we have had no word of Donald for a long time now, and all we can do is to keep hope in the front of our thoughts. He was a skilled and trusted performer, and of great personal qualities. No news may be good news, and we just wait patiently with you for some word. But in our hearts we find it difficult to dispel the encircling gloom. I'm sorry to have to tell you of our fears, but I know that you will bravely stand shoulder to shoulder with Amie and me here, and with John in distant parts, waiting and hoping in steadfast faith. Courage, Service and Sacrifice were as a part of Donald's being, and we are raised up and supported in the knowledge that he would do his job and leave the rest to the Fates. Daddy.'

George copied this portion of a letter received from his father into his scrapbook. He hadn't received their letters. Notice the use of the past tense, 'he was a skilled and trusted performer'. It must've been a terrible blow for George to read his father's words. 'Courage, Service and Sacrifice' were not just seen as Donald's values; they were at the core of who he was, his very being.

'Leave the rest to the Fates' – a reminder to accept what's within his control. Through the stand he took in the face of his unavoidable circumstances as a POW, demonstrating inner strength and resilience, George reframed it into an opportunity to focus on his purpose. He continued writing.

In a postcard dated 25 May 1942, George wrote: 'Spring is here too. Even here!' Having already taken exams as a POW in French and Spanish from the Royal Society of Arts and Institute of Linguists, he busied himself with his plan to get an honours degree from the University of London.

1 July 1942

From an essay on Malory's 'Morte d'Arthur'

'Now, said the King, I am sure at this quest of the Sancgreal shall all ye of the Table Round depart, and never shall I see you whole again together; therefore I will see you all whole together in the meadow of Camelot to joust and to tourney, that after your death men may speak of it that such good knights were shortly together such a day.'

The dreams that we remember of our childhood days when we lived so vividly, the carefree active life, are recalled in these sunny pages. Irresistibly we are made to think of the destruction of the flower of chivalry in 1918, in 1942.

The conflict of WW2 shattered the stability of many nations, disrupted social structures and challenged the ideals of civilisation. The parallels made between Camelot and 20th-century war-torn Europe reflect the collapse of idealised order, strife and betrayal and the loss of chivalric values. George's father spoke of courage, service, sacrifice and bravery – all recognised as qualities of honour and heroism.

Extract from a postcard dated 13 July 1942

Dear Mr Kerr

Here the chaps are in fine health and as 'brown as berries'. When I last wrote you we had nine of 9/3 Section. Now we are 8!! Brown escaped on June 23 and is now interned in the south of France, along with lots of other fellows. The eight remaining here are Henderson, Richards, Oxley, Green, Griffin, Perry, Cruddas and myself.

We are 54 here now and I am in complete charge of the camp, working directly under the Swiss Officer. He is not too bad. I wish you were here with us.

The last two years have been long, haven't they? Perhaps much more for you than me. Gough is better again now but still away from camp.

Best wishes. Cheerio. S Davies.

More positive correspondence from Corporal Stan Davies, showing how important it was for them to stay in touch with one another. Separated yet still connected, friendship was prioritised.

14 July 1942

From an essay on William Cowper

'The Task' embraces every aspect of the man; the nature lover, Evangelist, invalid, moralist, poet. Cowper is an acute observer of everything.

Accurately, then, towards the closing lines of 'The Task', he sets down on paper what he believes to be the purpose of his life. In his search for the meaning in all his suffering, he unwittingly gives us what we may value as highly.

'He is the happy man, whose life e'en now
shows somewhat of that happier life to come;
who doom'd to an obscure but tranquil state,
is pleased with it, and, were he free to choose,
would make his fate his choice.'

In this entry, the extract covers what Cowper perceived to be the purpose of his life, a realisation he'd arrived at through his own search for meaning in his suffering, that true happiness is found in the contentment and acceptance of your present circumstances. In including it here, George acknowledged his responsibility and ability to search for his own meaning in life.

George's scrapbook doesn't record this, but on 23 July 1942 George received a letter from his father finally announcing that the official record on Donald is 'previously reported missing, now presumed killed in action'. His following letter carried a much more cheerful and supportive tone.

> **Extract from a letter dated 5 August 1942 from his father**
> Dear George
> As to any sense of despondency that besets you, our constant marvel is that you keep even a shade of cheerful outlook. We have no thoughts about you except of your wellbeing, now and later on. Whatever you think best, it will be my utmost endeavour to support and encourage.
>
> All I meant to imply was that you were tackling a lot of study, and I didn't want you to overdo work. I think the project is most enterprising and ambitious, but possible. As it is certainly a high standard of objective, difficult of attainment even in the best environment, I wanted you to know that we understood the difficulties and that neither you nor we were to be downcast for a minute if you didn't ring the bell at your first attempt. But as I said to you before you left in Xmas 1939, always keep in the forefront of your thoughts at all times, and for all time, or for all my time rather, I am with you all the way, wherever it leads, and that no power in Heaven or Earth can keep my heart and my hand from being as your very own in your cause. You have done well.
> Cheerio. Love from Daddy.

If George had felt he needed permission to pursue his own 'Way of Life', this letter would've brought him great comfort knowing he had his father's full support.

I recall receiving a similarly reassuring letter when planning my next steps after graduation and applying for jobs.

Extract from a letter dated 20 November 1995
Dear Amy

Don't be too easily put off by rejection or no answer at all. You'll finally walk it. I thought you said something about trying to impress me/us. No need to. We have every confidence in a marvellously performing girl. You have certainly been doing a lot of reading and you write very fluently and well.

Let me know how else I can help.

Love George

Create: Reflections with Actions

↗ MEANINGFUL BEAUTY

Nurturing your inner beauty is a pathway to a more meaningful life. Society often fixates on external appearances, so developing internal qualities such as empathy, gratitude, resilience and self-love allows your inner beauty to radiate outwardly. Prioritising inner growth and self-care will set you on a transformative journey that both nourishes your soul and enhances your capacity to contribute positively to the world. Embracing life's journey with all its twists and turns will reveal the true beauty and the unwavering spirit within you. Reflect on the moments in your everyday life where beauty exists and consider what changes you can make to invite even more.

↗ NO LIMITATIONS

Your choices determine what you believe is possible. Take a moment to imagine a life with no limitations on your achievements. Whether it's creating something, exploring new places or helping others in meaningful ways, know you're surrounded by people supporting and inspiring you to make it happen. You sense freedom, possibility and tranquillity. In this limitless life, you're living in alignment with your values and passions, making a positive impact on the world, addressing the causes and issues that deeply resonate with you, using your unique gifts and strengths to create meaningful change.

You can see how you've played a significant role in resolving challenges. Your contributions to the world made a difference. You've engaged in activities that brought joy and fulfilment. You've empowered others and created a lasting legacy of compassion and service. In detail, write down everything that is possible, knowing that there are no limitations. What did you make happen? Where were you? What were you doing? Who were you with? Where were you living? Use your aspirations to help choose long-term intentions that will form the direction of your plan.

✈ LETTER FROM BEYOND

In my early forties, after drafting my will, I privately penned my first Letter from Beyond – a goodbye note to family and friends sharing reflections, achievements and gratitude. Updating it annually helps me focus on meaningful, purposeful activities and provides me with reassurance, knowing I've left a personal letter to those I love to inspire them to live with purpose. Have you taken responsibility for your own future? If tomorrow were your last day, would your current activities align with your aspirations? How would you prefer to choose to spend your remaining time? To plan a purposeful life, prioritise what really matters and leave a beautiful, meaningful message for those you've left behind, write your Letter from Beyond.

Create: Celebrate and Continue

✈ ALPHA WAVE ACTIVATION

How can simple activities such as taking a shower, watching raindrops trickle down a windowpane or observing flickering flames enhance creativity? These moments of relaxation and quietness, also known as divergent thinking, when your mind is alert yet calm and not actively processing information, are often associated with alpha brainwave production and have been linked to improved creativity, learning, focus and stress reduction (Rani & Rao 1996; Sobolewski et al 2011). To channel this creative potential, allow your mind to wander freely; however, don't use all the hot water in anticipation of that inspirational shower moment!

Step 5: Create – Summary

Understand the transformative power of purpose to drive change. By reframing a crisis as the catalyst for a new beginning, you generate the opportunity to create what comes next. Drawing from years of experiences and learnings, harness your unique talents, gifts and strengths to spark conversations, instigate collaboration and inspire action.

Step 6: Collaborate

Collaborate to amplify impact: connect with purpose-driven individuals who share your values to pool resources and expertise to create a united community.

As Frederika Roberts shared in FOW 46, 'Positive Psychology', 'People matter and relationships matter. The quality of our relationships with other people impacts on our mental health, on our physical health and on how long we live, so it's really important.' As 'The Happiness Speaker', her approach focuses on giving people practical, evidence-based tools, 'applying science and research to what makes people tick and what makes them well. Part of being well is also about creating a better world and creating a better environment around ourselves, so positive psychology helps individuals and society flourish by leading connected, meaningful and fulfilled lives.'

You can make a difference on your own but the real magic happens when you're united around a common purpose. American professor, researcher and storyteller Brené Brown (2020) defines connection as 'the energy that exists between people when they feel seen, heard and valued; when they can give and receive without judgement; and when they derive sustenance and strength from the relationship'.

So, while you may seek individuality and recognition, going it alone will only ever take you so far. Thriving comes from the inter-dependence of collaboration and connection. Purposeful human collaboration beautifully mirrors the interconnectedness that exists effortlessly everywhere in nature, where different species collaborate to thrive within an ecosystem.

In FOW 314, 'Peace and Light', Nadine Hack emphasised responsible leadership, human rights, diversity and sustainability, believing we're all inextricably connected as one human family through the Ubuntu concept of 'I am because you are'. Nadine stressed the significance of sustaining meaningful connections and how we achieve more when cooperating with others as the 'whole is always greater than the sum of its parts. Synergy advances individual and collective goals. We're stronger together.'

Your connections and collaborations significantly influence how effective you'll be in pursuing your purpose and creating change in the world. Working with the right people accelerates and amplifies your efforts, increasing the likelihood of achieving your intentions. Sharing your purpose and why attracts the support you need to make it a reality. Collectively achieve your individual intentions through the transformative power of pooling resources to leverage skills, strengths and knowledge.

Don't just look for like-minded people either: look for those who bring to the table what you don't. In FOW 185, 'Queen of Behaviours', Vicky O'Farrell said, 'It's about recognising, understanding and respecting our differences because we all have a place in this world and we all have value to bring. It's understanding if I'm going to be on a project, if I'm going to work and do something, who do I need around me that's going to help me make this a success?'

My participation in multiple business mastermind groups has underscored how collective efforts create a shared mind to demonstrate how purposeful collaboration forms the necessary synergy to spark creativity, innovation and solutions. Expanding both my professional and personal networks has opened doors to new connections, leading to more opportunities for collaboration and amplifying our collective impact.

In FOW 347, 'Heartfelt Connection', Gill Tiney's purpose is clear: to teach the world to collaborate. Her mission involves connecting people and showing them a path away from fear, scarcity and competition towards love, connection and abundance. Through her business community, Gill has created a collaborative culture that encourages a space for abundant, solution-focused thinking where members are empowered to contribute meaningfully, deliver knowledge, promote growth and work together to create a better world.

Volunteering exemplifies collaboration and purpose, as it involves collective action. I love sport, being outside, surrounded by beautiful countryside, sunny days and volunteering. For me, cricket ticks all of these boxes. From the age of eight, my brother Toby and I loved playing outside the boundary, venturing off to explore surrounding fields while Dad played and Mum did the scoring.

Reflecting fondly on these times, in the summer of 2011 I urged Jon to join a local cricket club while our children were still young. I wanted them to experience community spirit, freedom of exploration and the joy of being active all day. A cricket club embodies true collaboration, bringing together players of all ages, abilities and backgrounds to form and play as one team. Few sports match this level of inclusivity and diversity. Beyond sport, it offers a community, for the players, their families, friends, spectators and all the dedicated volunteers who manage the club and maintain the grounds.

In November 2011, elected to the cricket club's committee, I sought ways to boost membership numbers. That's when I stumbled across NatWest CricketForce (NWCF). Inspired by TV shows such as *DIY SOS, Changing Rooms* and *Ground Force,* NWCF combined volunteering with DIY-style improvements. After researching the club's immediate resources and connections, it became evident that we already had everything we required for growth; however, it was only a few club 'legends' who were actively making a difference.

Our NWCF collaborative success stemmed from a clear vision, a detailed plan and a strong focus on objectives – a Purpose, a Plan and a Focus on Why. This formula exemplifies how to collaborate and share purpose effectively as once these steps were taken, momentum quickly built providing a pathway for others to contribute enthusiastically.

After we had inspired and mobilised more than 150 volunteers, the facilities of the cricket club were enhanced, its visibility amplified and its membership increased. With contributions from more than 50 local and national companies, plus skilled and unskilled volunteer hours, the estimated savings and donations totalled £36,000. Being part of the invaluable transformation gave everyone a great sense of community spirit. It wasn't just about renovations; it was about creating group enthusiasm for the project, making the club the hub of the community, and having a lot of fun in the process.

In October 2012, I received an Outstanding Service to Cricket Award (OSCA) at Lord's Cricket Ground for making a positive and sustainable impact on a cricket club, going beyond the call of duty, galvanising club members and providing a legacy of future stability and growth for the club and the community. My enthusiasm had inspired commitment and confidence in others.

However, while I may have been the award's named recipient, the project's success was achieved through a collaborative effort, with all club members contributing. More than a decade later, the cricket club continues to thrive from the extraordinary volunteer efforts demonstrating the priceless value of community involvement. Jon, Holly and Eddie all play cricket and our family remains deeply connected to this community, showcasing how cricket continues to unite families across generations.

Volunteering and fundraising have always been integral to my life's purpose, inspired by my parents' and grandparents' community involvement. From walking my elderly neighbour's dog at age eight, to coaching rowing for visually impaired and blind children as a teenager, to being a Team Leader Games Maker at the London 2012 Olympic Games, to organising large rugby festivals and tours, each experience has brought me joy and fulfilment. Jon shares this passion, volunteering at parkruns, as an emergency courier blood runner, a cricket club committee member and managing county-level rugby. Holly and Eddie also embrace volunteering and fundraising, aligning their passions with their strengths.

Extending beyond volunteering, collaboration is integral in all areas of life – the workplace, the home, educational settings, sports teams, communities and nations. Deeply embedded in daily life, it's essential for innovation, progress and evolution. Supportive, positive, purpose-driven people make themselves open to the opportunity to build and nurture valued relationships, and are willing to plant seeds that will eventually flourish to produce fruit. Planning and building your collaborative network may require time, effort and patience. However, there's nothing more important in life than the relationships you choose to nurture.

George's Scrapbook
6 September 1942 – May 1943

Extract from a postcard sent 5 June 1942
Dear Amie & Daddy
Summary of programmes:
1. Gain exemption by writing of my 2 certs. from London Matric.
2. Sit the Inter Arts London External in Nov. 1942 in English, English History, French & Latin.
3. Having passed that, begin more intensive studies for Final BA London to be taken in Nov. '43 or Spring '44, and at the same time if possible attempt also the Oxford special course for POWs in English.

With a clear purpose and a determined action plan, George recruited support from his external network to get all he needed to succeed.

6 September 1942
'Remember that this is not a misfortune, but that to bear it nobly is good fortune.' Marcus Aurelius

'But I will put you in prison. Man, what are you saying? You may put my body in prison, but my mind not even Zeus himself can overpower.' Epictetus

'The fly – a black incarnation of freedom.' John Ruskin

'A counted number of pulses only is given to us of a variegated, aromatic life. How may we see in them all that is to be seen by the finest senses? How can we pass most swiftly from point to point, and be present always at the focus where the greatest number of vital forces unite in their purest energy? To burn always with this hard, gem-like flame, to maintain this ecstasy, is success in life. While all melts under our feet we may well catch at any exquisite passion, or any contribution to knowledge, that seems, by a lifted horizon, to set the spirit free for a moment.' Walter Pater

'Glory is after all the thing which has the best chance of not being altogether vanity.' Renan

'For what doth the Lord require of thee, but to do justly, to love mercy, and to walk humbly with thy God.' Micah

'They [the Greeks] are deceased. They are said to be immortal, because they have written a good epitaph; but they are gone.' Bagehot on Cowper

Misfortune paradoxically provides the opportunity for growth. Essayist and art critic Walter Pater emphasises the importance of creating, fully experiencing and appreciating fulfilling moments, not simply filling them in. Inspiration from French philosopher Ernest Renan, the Bible, and English journalist Walter Bagehot offer further reflection on what really matters, on fundamental principles and values, and on the temporal nature of human existence.

Collectively these lines form a powerful 'Way of Life' for George to follow: a reminder of what you can and can't control; that true freedom lies within your thoughts, your attitudes and your judgements; that even in the direst of circumstances, you still possess agency, freedom and autonomy of thought. Despite his physical body being held captive, his mind was liberated to explore whatever he chose.

11 September 1942
Notes and quotations – 'The Miraculous Birth of Language' by Professor Richard Albert Wilson
'In each isolated piece of matter which makes up a man's body, there is centred a power which radiates to the furthest boundaries of space and time.'
'The task set to man, then, on emerging into possession of this

new world of conscious mind, was to "intellect" the world, to take mental possession of it, to transfer its types one by one from the outward space-time world of nature to the inner space-time world of mind.'

'In nature there are only two fundamental generic types, corresponding to the two sense media, space and time: Form is the natural expression of space; Sound is the natural and direct expression of time.'

'Written language is a conventional and not a natural art, addressing itself to the imagination and not the senses.'

Reflecting on Wilson's book, George wrote him a letter sharing his insights. Throughout life, George continued this practice, writing to people who inspired him, often receiving wonderful typed or handwritten responses from people such as actor Laurence Olivier, politician Harold Wilson, golfer Tom Watson and even one from Michael Bond, author of the *Paddington* books, complete with bear paw inkblots.

Letter sent to US President Carter (undated)
Dear President Carter
A word of friendship and thanks to you from a small family in this country for all you have done and tried to do during your Presidency. Not only for the country, for the world.

It is perhaps an impertinence to address a Head of State in this way, perhaps naive to feel that it is worth doing. But many things are left unsaid in life – 'thank you' most frequently – and the gap they leave can seem to yawn.

In brief we feel that a good man has done a fine job. It would be a pity if, because that sentence were not written and despatched to you, that your worth and effort had not been valued and appreciated.

Please, therefore accept this as the hand of friendship extended to you and to your wife from six of us on this side of the Atlantic.

George, Ruth, Catharine, Tony, Amy and Toby

On 12 September 1942, George was transferred to Oflag VII B, Eichstätt, describing it in his July 1945 entry.

Eichstätt had stumbled on the Warburg-hut formula. But here the buildings were laid tidily side by side, and on a spring evening, with grey ribbons of smoke rising from every chimney vertically to the sky, the lower camp resembled a Welsh mining village. On the bank above, the remainder of the prisoners were housed in tall, unremarkable buildings.

In the final year, when our air forces were able to bomb and did bomb, we were anxious that our camp should not be mistaken for what it had previously been, a German barracks. It had approximately the area of a greyhound track, and at night, with the lamps blazing along the perimeter, illuminating the track surround and leaving a deep pool of dark in the centre, we recalled the appearance of White City.

Eichstätt could boast the remains of a small Roman camp, which had served as an outpost against the Barbarians during the campaigns of Marcus Aurelius in Southern Germany. Grass grew now over the walls, and wild strawberries had rooted between the stones. Below, the river moved by as silently now as then. Here, a soldier, a philosopher, might well have written something of his meditations. 'Men seek out for themselves, cottages in the country, lovely sea-shores and mountains'.

Shortly after this move, George received devastating news.

Extract from a letter dated 21 September 1942
My Dear George,
I hope you have received my last letter to you, telling you of your daddy's operation. I must tell you that he died this morning, suddenly, having improved slightly after a magnificent struggle for life such as only he could make. Now, you must never feel that you are without a home. Such as I can, I will have one

for you, for you to look upon and feel about as your own.

I fear this is all a terrible blow to you, and all I can say or do is to repeat that you will always have a home, and that I will always be behind you and back you up in all your endeavours, decisions and actions. You will be very proud to read the letters I have already had from people about your daddy.

Bye-bye, all my love from Amie.

George has now lost his brother and father.

25 September 1942
War: Over the sleeping, tented fields of Europe, the notes of the Reveille stir a reluctant world to the impossible conflict.

30 September 1942
Proposal to write 'Way of Life' to meet the need for a planned life, to meet every circumstance of life, every facet of living.

Here's that line in context, and perhaps now you can understand just how profound it was for me to encounter George's proposal to write about navigating life's challenges in his scrapbook, 80 years after its inception, given the work I focus on today.

5 October 1942
Tolerance in prison: the trouble is that one cannot conscientiously tell oneself on passing a group of people that one will never see them again.

How unsettling to have lived like this every day.

6 October 1942
A dream: (Worried greatly because I had been accused of fratricide, though remembering neither the incentive nor the deed itself. Worried too by my inability to prove my innocence, and appalled

by the threat of hanging. I could not understand, as I remarked to a friend, how they could believe that I had killed Donald. Admittedly, he was no longer with the living. Certainly, he had disappeared, but then he was dead; he had been shot down in a Blenheim patrol over the Channel. How absurd to accuse me of killing someone already dead! At any rate, I assured myself, it will all be cleared up when I awake.)

Woke up; and of course, Donald is dead.

Remember George once referred to Donald as Icarus and the subsequent regret he felt almost a year ago in November 1941? It's clearly still haunting him.

7 October 1942

Reading: During my first 20 years I read widely and indiscriminately (amongst the great ones, mind you, but without purpose). And the slower process now of careful study, guided always by instinct and critical awareness, is an attempt to correct earlier faults. Presumably the end should be a water colour, good or bad – according to the man himself, in which these recurrent courses of reading are the primary and secondary washes. Finally there will be the deeper tones of detail with here and there, of course, evidence of the tricks of the trade, stippling, dry-point and pencil drawing, the idiosyncrasies of the individual.

His reading reflects his desire for his future contribution to his chosen craft, speaking of his knowledge and understanding of art, life and how to convey his message. Focused on his aspirations, he uses all available time. The seed is planted; now he's putting his purpose and plan into action.

Extract from a letter received 17 March 1943 from Vancouver BC, Canada

Dear Lieutenant Kerr,

Am glad you found some 'excitement' from the book in your present restricted mode of life. Every parcel of mental liberation that comes your way in your present circumstances must be a net gain. I am glad that my small volume added something to the general store. When I got your card it struck me as odd how a book, once off the press, travels in all directions and turns up on occasion in the most unexpected places.

The book grew out of class lectures and took shape slowly and without long into book form. I got a good deal of pleasure in the making and experienced a number of quiet thrills in the discovery of new things about language, evolution and human life. Glad when I find a response from others.

Very sincerely, R A Wilson

A reply from Wilson, the author George had mentioned on 11 September 1942, not only reinforces 'mental liberation', it details a clear plan of how to amplify a message through the written word to influence, impact and inspire people globally. A seed is planted.

May 1943

Let us stay – shall we? – at this moment in time,
without motion, either of us, casually watching
at the world slipping and spinning and falling;
Tranquil, two of us, negligent, watchful,
you with your head half turned, and I,
indulgent, stooping for a rhyme.

In preparation for his exams, George sent Amie a postcard on 26 July 1943 requesting anything the University of London 'might consider helpful to an external student, without a tutor, but a fairly well-stocked library' and then shared his progress with Amie a week later.

Extract from a letter dated 1 August 1943

Dear Amie

I have, during the last month, sacrificed much – well for this place, at any note! Rather than depart from my routine. There has been music each night, which I have had to miss. All the flowers have blossomed and I have longed to try to paint some, but have not dared to spend the time. And then I have not done any writing. Well – I mean to make up for this. I mean, too, to plan as if for July '44, so that I shall make no mistake with that exam. My French must be developed. I may join a French speaking mess – Canadians, live with them for six months. I mean to keep steadily at my English (& Latin, tho' I shall not need it for the exam) and at my writing. As recreation, in a strictly subordinate position I shall put my play action, painting and music. So much for my dreams and schemes.

George

Through collaboration, expertise leveraged, he focused on his plan.

Collaborate: Reflections with Actions

↗ MEANINGFUL PLANNING

Family comes first. Block out and protect dedicated family time well in advance, then review the upcoming months and weeks allocating time for meaningful activities. Each morning, prioritise tasks based on their significance to ensure you remain focused on your Desire Path.

↗ YOU OR WHO?

Clarify your intentions by detailing the why, what, when, who, where and how. Develop a focused action plan with purposeful intentions and milestones. Celebrate every step connected to your purpose but, before you take any action, think – you or who? To amplify results, identify necessary collaborators and delegate tasks to those with more relevant expertise, freeing you to focus on your gifts, passions and strengths.

↗ THANK YOU, THANK YOU, THANK YOU!

As George wrote in his letter to President Carter, don't leave things unsaid. Express gratitude often and observe the positive impact it has on both yourself and others. Saying thank you and accepting compliments builds trust, rapport and stronger relationships, enhances self-esteem, keeps you present and triggers the release of the feel-good neurotransmitters serotonin and dopamine. Be grateful, say thank you, say it often!

Collaborate: Celebrate and Continue

↗ LIBERATE YOUR MIND

To feel more empowered and open to new possibilities, prioritise joy. Identify what brings you joy, love and connection and break free from negative thought patterns, limiting beliefs or any emotional burdens that are restricting you. At the end of each day, celebrate moments of mental liberation for enhanced wellbeing and personal growth.

Step 6: Collaborate – Summary

Collaborating towards a common purpose brings fulfilment and achievement. Shift the focus from what the world can do for you to what you can do for the world. Define what you want to create, the world you envision and who you need to make it happen. Seek collaboration to bring your purpose to life and connect with purpose-driven individuals who share your values to create a united community, amplifying your impact on what matters most. When you Focus on Why, the rest falls into place.

PART 2: PLAN – Summary

Do your Why and Purpose statements now need updating? Review them to ensure that your purpose, plan and intentions are fully aligned. A well-crafted plan of action serves as your roadmap, empowering you to move forward with purpose. By making conscious choices and identifying your collaborators, your plan transforms abstract goals into tangible steps, offering you clarity on your life journey. It lays the foundation for collaboration, moving an individual purpose to become shared and united. Chart your meaningful life and collaborate with others for a purpose-driven journey infused with intention and joy.

PART 3
FOCUS

Focus on Why
Step 7: Commit wholeheartedly with unwavering focus
Step 8: Contribute to create positive ripple effects
Step 9: Change with your evolving purpose

Armed with your purpose and a plan, now it's time to focus. With life's complexities, while starting with your why is crucial, maintaining a constant focus on it is essential as it provides you with a source of power, persistence and drive. By filtering out distractions, focus enables effective decision-making, helping you align appropriate actions with purposeful intentions. Your predominant focus shapes your actions, ultimately defining your life trajectory. Reflect on where you allocate your time and energy to identify activities that ignite your passion and vitality, and prioritise what truly matters to pave the way for your purposeful path.

Step 7: Commit

Commit wholeheartedly with unwavering focus: using your why as your intrinsic driving force, take responsibility for your decisions and actions to pursue your purpose with courage, resilience and grit.

Daily commitment to a purpose gives you a greater sense of meaning and significance in life and contributes to your wellbeing. Committing to continuous personal growth will open doors to so many opportunities. Through the challenges and obstacles you face, along with lessons gained from the commitments you make, you'll achieve the freedom you desire. If you ever doubt your ability to make a difference, remember that all change is driven by the words or actions of individuals. Each person has the capacity to be remarkable. Stay true to yourself, align your values with your work and surround yourself with people who support and uplift you.

What actions are you committed to today that will lead you towards a more purposeful life of contribution, service and meaning? As life is filled with family, work, study, health and personal development commitments, it's crucial to fully understand the implications involved before making a commitment, as they're founded on trust and dedication. With few exceptions, such as serious events, illness or uncontrollable circumstances, I uphold commitments I make. How often do you honour yours?

While some commitments may feel constraining, what if you were to find freedom through them instead? The discipline of consistency is often undervalued, yet it's integral to success. As everything is interconnected, how you approach one thing reflects how you approach everything. Consistently delivering quality over time is paramount as your actions shape your life, with daily actions holding more weight than occasional ones. Consistency turns the everyday ordinary into the extraordinary.

Consider the accomplishments seen at the Olympic and Paralympic Games. Athletes commit to rigorous training and preparation, emphasising the focus on consistency and quality. Not everyone wins a medal, but they earn the right to call themselves Olympians or Paralympians through their dedication. Beginning as ordinary individuals, they transform into extraordinary athletes through their unwavering, focused commitment!

When I launched the podcast, *Focus on WHY,* my intention was, and remains, to inspire, enable and empower listeners to focus on their purpose and achieve self-fulfilment. Using this platform to share their commitment publicly, each guest brings a unique experience to the podcast. Through their passion and dedication to a cause, their stories benefit all who tune in. Ensuring others don't face the same challenges they've endured, their commitment is deeply meaningful, often moving them, me and listeners to tears.

Whether personally experienced or witnessed, pain often drives the why and helps people to focus and commit to solving that problem for others. Recognising their unique responsibility to honour their purpose, they reshape their beliefs and correct past circumstances. These catalysts of pain, disappointment, anger, frustration, absence or injustice provide them with powerful motivation to act and commit to their life's work.

Dr Susanna Petche (FOW 366, 'Healing with Purpose') draws from years of clinical practice, personal experience and academic knowledge to fulfil her purpose of educating the public and medical professionals about the existence and consequences of psychological trauma. With vulnerability and courage, she shares her story, offering hope for others to use their experiences as a 'catalyst for the next phase of their life'.

What's holding you back from committing to your purpose? It's likely linked to a fear. Embracing your purpose empowers you to move beyond fear. Connecting to a reason greater than yourself reveals the futility of unnecessary worry. Shifting from fear-based to purpose-focused motivation, you're able to commit to an impact-focused mission and vision, prioritising serving others over just yourself. As a result, the entire world benefits. Doing what you love and what's important, surrounded by the right people and engaged in meaningful activities, helps you create harmony and makes everyday life worth living. As results accumulate, your confidence grows, and you become more empowered by your purpose.

In FOW 277, 'Students Against Sexism', university students Camille, Kelvina and Harini courageously spoke out against sexism, recognising that individual voices become more powerful when unified. Advocating for their beliefs, transforming their negative experiences into positive action, and united in solidarity by their mission they're committed to achieving gender equality. Reflect on your sense of unity with others on topics you strongly believe in.

If you encounter something in life that angers you, causes you great pain or deeply troubles you, instead of saying that somebody really should do something to change that, consider what actions you could take to effect that change yourself. What situation would you like to resolve? What challenges do you face that will inspire you to fight for justice, peace or resolution? Focus on finding solutions to challenges that are meaningful to you.

In FOW 215, 'Time for a Change', Shelley Bridgman shared the belief that everyone is put on the planet for a purpose. Each individual has a reason for being here. Having changed gender, she faced restrictions that prevented her from being legally recognised as female while maintaining her marriage. As a result, she was instructed to annul the marriage, a step she was unwilling to take. Shelley stood firm in her beliefs. In 2019, after an 11-year fight, Shelley emerged victorious against the UK government in the European Court of Justice, profoundly impacting thousands of lives across Europe.

Daily persistence and deliberate practice lead to mastery. It's the seemingly inconsequential, more mundane actions that compound over time and make a significant difference. Clarity of purpose helps you understand why these daily actions matter. Mastering the mundane translates to mastering life and is applicable to business and personal areas. Commitment to daily habits, decisions and choices determines your future. Ultimately, every moment influences your life's work and trajectory.

Nurture your talents, relationships and dreams and allow them to flourish and evolve. Your thoughts are potential seeds and it's up to you which ones you nurture or discard. For you to harvest, first you must make the effort to plant seeds.

My grandmother Ruth's legacy of kindness, compassion and generosity speaks to the power of her actions and their lasting impact. A neighbour's response to my mother's surprise at the large numbers of people attending Ruth's funeral highlighted this: 'But Ruth was lovely. You reap what you sow.'

In relation to trust, hope and growth, the metaphor of seeds resonates. Like seeds, dreams, intentions and possibilities hold immense potential to dramatically evolve, symbolising life's journey of change and transformation. While planted in the present, they simultaneously embody the future. The transformation of a tiny seed into something incredible illustrates what's possible when all the right conditions align.

In creating my podcast, I'd not only planted a seed to grow but also provided the nourishment necessary for someone else's seed growth. I received this message from a nurse from Amsterdam: 'Loving it. It is the water to a seed I planted that is desperate to grow but is still finding its roots. Talking in metaphors is so much easier. Taking it all in to grow, improve and explore my work and thinking of what new roads to explore. So very inspiring. Thanks.'

The discipline of consistent, intentional action is the bridge from dream to reality; determination and a will to win are prerequisites for success. In FOW 5, 'The Art of Social Selling', Sam Rathling said that habits are really important: 'It's about being consistent and showing up, being visible and demonstrating your credibility.' Sam focuses on the importance of daily consistency despite adversity and challenges, saying in business and life there's always going to be 'ups and downs but the growth happens in the valleys'.

Don't underestimate where you apply your focus within your daily routine. How you spend your time reflects what you prioritise and demonstrates commitment in your life. If your life lacks fulfilment, examine how you spend your time and make the necessary adjustments. To truly make a difference in the world, commitment is key. The meaningful emotional significance you attach to your purpose serves as a powerful motivator to sustain your commitment and dedication – it's your Focus on Why.

In almost every single podcast episode I've recorded, guests have discussed how they wish to create a meaningful, positive impact during their lifetime and leave behind a lasting legacy for generations to come. In FOW 333, 'The Gift of Sight', entrepreneur Paul Dunn focused on two intentions: deliver amazing value to those he was privileged to serve, and have fun doing it. Then Paul shared the question he'd been asked which subsequently changed the course of his life: 'What if every time you do business, something great happens in the world?' So, now there's a third intention: that something great happens in the world as a result. 'When your vision becomes more powerful than your memory, your future becomes more powerful than your past.'

Is your individual or business legacy one of consumption or of contribution? Corporations make valuable social impact, contributing directly and indirectly towards the sustainability of the planet and the wellbeing of all those who live on it; therefore every decision a company makes matters. Those who authentically lead with purpose through collaboration are not only changing the nature of how business is conducted and perceived by their consumers, but they're also responsible for the changing of nature itself. Gast et al (2020) emphasised that companies hold both an 'opportunity, and an obligation, to engage on the urgent needs of our planet'.

Authentic alignment is critical for companies claiming to have a strong sense of purpose and commitment to social and environmental causes. Without genuine integration into core business practices, instead of implementing meaningful change, they're found guilty of greenwashing or purpose-washing, using purpose in their marketing to create a positive image but with no real substance behind their sustainability claims.

However, seeing business as a force for good and moving towards greater responsibility, many for-profit companies are now choosing to become verified as a Certified B Corporation, where they need to meet very high standards of social and environmental performance, public transparency and legal accountability to balance profit and purpose. If every company adopted this level of commitment, accountability and understanding, the world of business would significantly contribute towards a better future for people and the planet.

George's Scrapbook
November 1943 – 10 March 1944

November 1943

If I should go beyond this world, I should be asked whence I had come. And if I were the first ever to have made such a journey, it would surely be for me to make the most of my former home, to tell these strangers not only its name but its nature, who its owners were, who dwelt there, how they dwell.

Thus I would end my story. And my hearers would feel not only the dissatisfaction the historian must give by his version of the truth, nor that which the geographer's image must promote, for both these are recognised compromises with reality, but dissatisfaction, too, with the lack of finish, the incompleteness of my story. I should have been speaking for many hours, they listening for as many. But suddenly, with my record of my last day in the world, my story would have stopped, all action magically held in suspense.

I should have spoken of men and events. I should have shown men striving with and against other men, events arising from and giving rise to other events; change acting upon condition, constancy again counteracting change. But condition always remaining. They would have noticed this permanence of condition and they would naturally have enquired into its nature. What they would have found, those qualities of the world which they would have agreed to be permanent, would have been life and death. They would have seen too that death itself was but another aspect of life, and that, therefore, life alone was permanent.

But the endlessness not only of individual lives but of life itself, whereby death, which might reasonably have been held its end, is denied that function and becomes merely its latest aspect, this endlessness would have been so apparent throughout, that they would wish to question me further about my world, to enquire into its meaning for us who are of it, and for them who are strangers to it.

November 1943

> We are not dead, we who are living here,
> watching the snows cover the year,
> seeing the river freeze, and the wild trees
> tamed to a stiff repose.
>
> It is quiet here save for the blustering gale
> outside, the rattle of hail;
> moisture runs on the window-pane,
> and pages turn; the chair leg creaks again.

November 1943

I have pictured myself as telling the story of the world to people who are strangers to it, in order that I should be tempted to speak of it objectively. And I have shown myself as giving a record of man's life upon the world, and of the world seen through man's eyes because the enquiry is made by man for man, and because we are more familiar with man's life than with that of any other being.

I do not fail, therefore, to appreciate that the perception of the world and of life in it, is a human perception, that the world I speak of is my perception of the world and that my understanding of life – should I ever acquire one – would be, in fact, my understanding of my perception of life.

But these are complications which may profitably be studied after I have come to some understanding of my perception of life, or, as I mean for convenience to call it, my understanding of life.

I do not promise myself that I ever shall understand life. Indeed I write this in the belief that – I am, that Life is, and that I and life are related at all times in a way which I may often know intuitively, in part if not in whole, and that by the method and discipline imposed by this essay, I shall come to a more conscious recognition of this relationship. But by thus formulating my thought, I can only acquire for myself a sense of balance as it were; I cannot be said to have come any nearer an understanding of life. And at the beginning of this enquiry I am making, I must confess to this additional belief, that it is not possible for me or for anyone ever to understand life.

You will remember those strangers I was speaking to, who were puzzled by my account of the world. They felt the narrative to be unsatisfactory in some way, like my account of life in that world, unfinished. And I must agree with them. It was unfinished. Mine had been a base record of events and places and names. Of course I had mentioned such motives as I had thought might justifiably be associated with these actions.

All the complex statements had been reduced to the two words 'Life is'. Let us look more closely at this phrase 'Life is'. My listeners were dissatisfied with it as representing the conclusion to which all that I had been saying, led. But their dissatisfaction with it was as a conclusion which it is not. For every enquiry must start not end with these words. My listeners had expected some tangible solution to the problem of the world. They could not, at first, see that 'Life is' was not that solution, but rather the more explicit statement of the problem.

7 January 1944

January 7th was always a festival with us at home, because it was Donald's birthday. John and I were born on the same day in April, at an interval of five years however, and accordingly it lacked unity somehow, our day, John's friends being five years older than mine, and everyone being asked to celebrate at once my youth and his maturity.

But January 7th was easier. We had all kept back some goodwill from Christmas and Donald received it all. Also it was the last family holiday before we all went back to school. Also, Donald was the middle boy, not nasty and juvenile as I, not grave and growing up as John. No, instinctively, we recognised, all of us, that Donald was the best of us. Instinctively, not, of course consciously. How could we consciously acknowledge him 'best', when he quite obviously was not as 'clever' as George, nor as settled as John? Mind you, he had all

John's skill at games, and he managed to jump the painful, awkward, pompous search-after-knowledge period of the 16 year old. Yes, he was happy, carefree, irresponsible perhaps but good, good, good...

January 1944

Friendship: Two friends will get so close to each other that, at last one of them must cry out – 'Get away. You're too near. Give me air. Let me breathe.'

That in short is the tragedy of life, – if it is a tragedy to be blind and not know it, – if it is a tragedy to be blind where all might see if they chose. The other episodes of life are melodramas only, pathetic, vain searches after a fuller communication with God, with art, with nature, self, money, the world. What then must we do? To recognise the impossibility of complete communion is not to check in any way the urge towards it. Be whole, live the full life, aspire but accept it all, strive and yearn but accept also the strife and the yearning. Accept life.

Life and how to live it: Work and tire yourself out working, and in your work express yourself fully as you know.

Know friendship then qua friendship; not something leading to a further deeper knowledge. That is not possible. Friendship qua friendship. Oh life! Lovely, graceful.

These two entries on friendship and life encapsulate George's 'Way of Life' perfectly: understand friendship for what it truly is without seeking deeper meaning or ulterior motives and engage in authentic work, exert yourself fully using all your talents, gifts and strengths.

January 1944

So there you are, or there am I, living; and nothing can stop life – without stopping my own observation of life. So I think to myself 'I might as well see this out'. After all, nobody is quite so well placed for reporting upon the thought processes of me as I.

Out come the notebooks, but what about the selection I make? I record not everything, a selection from everything, but what strikes me, what is of value for me, what is important, stimulating, exciting, at the moment of thought.

Put down 'Prelude' or 'World Enough and Time' and say lovely and true and sad, but what must we do about it? Then you are saying of the world you live in that it is all this – lovely, true, sad and bewildering. You are bewildered by your own world. You are bewildered by your own father. You don't know him. You can't speak to him for you are not friends, you two. And do you still ask what you must do? I suggest you try friendship.

Life, death and listening to music: These still, dead masks! Row after row of them, eyes closed or open, heads bent or erect, hands folded on laps or safely held in pockets. These marble foreheads, chiselled lips, moulded napes. Ah, but these quick, these flashing minds!

Have you ever shaken tiny breadcrumbs upon a silver tray? Watched them form and re-form in intricate design, sudden part-nerships, dissolution and further combination? Now the salver is at rest and the crumbs move no more, are still. See them where they lie, here, here and here. And there again another – and again there. These then are crumbs, these men listening to music. That lined face, living for 30 years, is now at rest in now. That smooth and chubby cheek – of 23 – at rest. Lip at rest; moving eye veiled by its lid at rest.

So this is life.
Shake up that silver tray again, will you?
So this is life.
Again?
So this is life – and this – and this. So these are life.
Now put down the tray, gently. Now blow the crumbs on to the
    floor.
So this is – well, what?

This silver tray metaphor represents the randomness of life in the scheme of things. George's experiences of war, prison life and years of captivity have profoundly transformed him. No longer pursuing his former career direction as an accountant, instead he's wholeheartedly committed to becoming a writer. With a crystal-clear purpose and evident plan, he acknowledges and respects that everyone has their own 'Way of Life'. It is just a way, not *the* way. His course and perspective understood, now he's committed to it.

> **3 March 1944**
> **From E M Forster's 'Aspects of the Novel'**
> 'There seems something else in life beside time, something which may conveniently be called "value", something which is measured not by minutes or hours, but by intensity, so that when we look at our past it does not stretch back evenly, but piles up into a few notable pinnacles, and when we look at the future it seems sometimes a wall, sometimes a sun, but never a chronological chart.'
>
> 'Daily life is practically composed of two lives, the life in time and the life of values – "I only saw her for five minutes, but it was worth it".'
>
> 'The story narrates the life in time; the good novel includes the life by values as well.'

These entries highlight the significance of how even the briefest of encounters or experiences create profound impact through their emotional importance in terms of joy, fulfilment or progress.

> **4 March 1944**
> **Marcel Proust: 'Du côté de chez Swann'**
> 'No doubt they regarded aesthetic values as material objects which an unclouded vision could not fail to discern, without needing to have their equivalent in experience of life stored up and slowly ripening in one's heart.'

> **'A l'ombre des jeunes filles en fleurs'**
> 'The time which we have at our disposal every day is elastic; the passions that we feel expand it, those that we inspire contract it; and habit fills up what remains.'

These entrancing words echo everything George and I believe about living, underscoring the significance of prioritising purposeful, fulfilling moments and identifying what brings you joy.

> **March 1944**
> **Daylight raid on Germany:** This afternoon was a brilliantly cloudless day, the air crisp, no trace of breeze, everything, trees and grass frozen motionless, and white and graceful in the sun. The earth white, the sky a dome of egg-shell blue.
>
> The siren had gone some time ago, and now we saw our first Allied bombers, midges at a great height, 300 of them moving steadily across the world to their target; they, moving to fierce, joyous action, to burning, twisting, falling death many of them, and we, favoured spectators, idling away our global war in vicarious excitement and nervous flippancy.

> **10 March 1944**
> **Fin d'hiver '44**
> From beyond the wire the song of the linnet comes;
> even to us who are deep as our necks in mire,
> whose ears are choked with mud of a long desire,
> – eyes sunk in clay, lips which would pray
> braying with laughter –
> even to us
> whose thoughts gone scuttling after
> whose laughter after whose hollow thoughts
> follow and chase faster,
> even to us,
> we the deformed of face

who lie mis-shapen, our mouths only normal, agape
who barely breathe, and who twist
our grinning lips at a Hell and at a Heaven
we have gladly missed – or, having seen
have lied of,
– said there was nothing in it,
– denied,
even to us there comes this sudden linnet,
staying the tears of long, hysterical laughter,
to the mud and the mire and the weary clay of us bringing
the song from beyond the wire the linnet is singing.

In wartime birdsong continues to bring beauty.

Commit: Reflections with Actions

↗ Purpose-Driven Audit

Whenever my coaching clients complete this exercise, they're staggered by the insights. To help you recognise how even the briefest moments in your day can bring fulfilment and joy, conduct a purpose-driven audit. With roughly 100 hours per week available, after accounting for sleep and essential tasks, if you want to fulfil your purpose, every moment left counts. Break down your day into 15-minute intervals and for a week monitor all activities. Rate each activity on a scale of 0–10 based on how much fulfilment it brings you in relation to your purpose. Reflect on your findings to identify areas for improvement. To use your time more purposefully, group similar tasks together and set time limits to maximise efficiency.

↗ Somebody Really Should Do Something About...

Do you ever catch yourself saying, somebody really should do something about... [insert your concern or inspiration for change]? Instead of delegating responsibility, be the change you wish to see and commit to taking that action yourself today. That somebody could be, should be, needs to be you.

↗ Positive Intentions

Achieving meaningful intentions takes time, consistency and effort. This may require forming new habits, taking action and staying positive. Accountability is crucial too. Sharing your purpose and plan with others boosts accountability. Consider partnering with a peer or friend, or working with a coach or mentor, and publicly declare your intentions to strengthen your commitment.

Commit: Celebrate and Continue

✈ HALF THE DIFFERENCE

Nearly 30 years ago, Jon and I devised 'Half the Difference', a purposeful investment approach focused on deferred gratification and perseverance. It began late one evening in London when, exhausted after work and faced with the choice of taxi or Tube, we opted for the latter to save money. We committed to setting aside half the saved amount each time, using it for something special later. This practice of investing in future joy through present restraint continues to enrich our lives today. Try it out and celebrate your future today!

Step 7: Commit – Summary

Commitment means investing in your future in the present moment. Wholeheartedly commit yourself to your purpose with unwavering focus. Balance planning for the future with being present today. Begin by investing in yourself. Invest in your mindset, knowledge, wellbeing and health. Pause, reflect, adjust and refocus. What's your commitment for today?

Step 8: Contribute

Contribute to create positive ripple effects: acknowledge all the ways your meaningful actions contribute to making an impact, whether at a local, national or global level.

You could spend a lifetime chasing fulfilment only to realise it was attainable at any moment through purposeful contribution, as it's through such an act of giving that a reciprocal relationship is created. Positivity, joy and fulfilment ensue from the accomplishment of your purpose. Making a positive impact on someone else's life in times of need creates immense satisfaction, benefiting all involved. Not limited by boundaries, service is the universal language of compassion, empathy and love, which speaks directly to the heart and soul of humanity. By channelling your efforts, living with intention and committing to meaningful actions daily, fulfilment becomes a constant.

Contribution refers to the act of giving, facilitating progress or aiding advancement. Many individuals I've spoken to have expressed the fundamental drive to help or serve others – a core aspect of purposeful action – the desire to make a difference, add value or generate an impact often stemming from a need to belong or to feel significant.

Inclusion and leadership specialist Jackie Handy encourages leaders to think and act differently, resulting in personal fulfilment as well as an engaged workforce. In FOW 129, 'Unconscious Competence', Jackie said, 'Belonging is something that is felt. You cannot simply say to somebody, "You are being included." They have to feel that within; they have to feel safe to open up to people around them about who they are. They have to feel valued for their contribution.'

Belonging to a supportive community provides a wealth of benefits, including fulfilment, acceptance, inclusion, safety, self-worth and a sense of being valued for your contributions. When connecting to something bigger than yourself, whether that's through your contribution, a cause you support or a commitment you make, not only do others benefit but it contributes to your own health and wellbeing.

In FOW 224, 'Being Human', distilling wisdom from global leaders,

Gary Hosey highlighted the importance of self-awareness and the roles intelligence quotient (IQ) and emotional quotient (EQ) have in the workplace and everyday life. He demonstrated how IQ and EQ achieve peak performance, motivation, relationship building, decision making, coping strategies and effective communication. To further enhance workplace productivity and satisfaction, Cranston & Keller (2013) recommended implementing a third critical element alongside IQ and EQ – meaning quotient (MQ).

Yet despite this rise of meaning, purpose and value on the employee and business agendas, and the establishment of purpose-driven cultures centred on sustainability, collaboration and community, many people remain unfulfilled, disengaged from their work and disconnected from their personal or business purpose. This low employee engagement exacts a high cost on business, leading to reduced productivity. Focused on employee wellbeing and engagement, Gallup's State of the Global Workplace 2023 Report revealed that not thriving at work can affect other aspects of life, including family relationships and described low engagement as 'enough to make the difference between success and a failure for humanity'. Their solution? 'Change the way your people are managed.'

With 40 years' experience of creating transformative teams, Adrian Brown (FOW 2, 'Stop, Pause, Breathe, Continue') said, 'We've got to change, and we've got to invent a future, but to do that, we've got to unlearn our past or uninvent our past. We're past-based creatures.' Returning in FOW 389, 'Creating Conditions for Growth', Adrian said, 'You've got to grow people. You've got to create the conditions for people to grow. That's what I've always done and when I'm not doing it, it fails.'

Zeno's Strength of Purpose study (2020) highlighted that global consumers are 'four to six times more likely to trust, buy, champion and protect companies with a strong purpose over those with a weaker one'. While 94 per cent of consumers say that purpose is important, only 37 per cent believe companies have a clear and strong purpose. Zeno calls this the 'Purpose Paradox' and concludes with challenging businesses to not just ask why they exist but to question their strength of purpose.

Deloitte (Corduneanu et al 2022) defined purpose as 'an organisation's explicit drive to create value beyond profit, specifically for our planet and the people on it,' stating that the 'most successful businesses of the future, those most appreciated by workers and consumers alike, will be those who deliver profit with purpose'. However, they identified five 'purpose gaps' between what employees desired and experienced.

In their research, McKinsey & Co (2020) stated that while 'contributing to society and creating meaningful work' were the two top priorities of employees, they'd also discovered purpose gaps. Their proposal to 'bridge a purpose gap' was to 'embed your reflection, exploration, discussion and action in the heart of your business and your organisation'. So, Reflection with Action isn't just an individual practice to craft a purposeful life – it appears it's an essential process for business operations too.

When you prioritise your contribution, you shift the focus of how you show up to work from merely completing tasks to actively advancing the vision and mission of the collective purpose. One global study (Malnight et al 2019) shared how when a defined purpose is placed at the core of its strategy, the benefits contribute towards a more unified business, more motivated stakeholders, more profitable growth and broader impact. Their recommendation was that purpose should not be seen as a 'one-off effort' to guide strategy, but to maintain constant assessment through 'sustained focus'.

Do you value, and are you valued for, your contribution? Sharing your purpose, vision and mission aligned with your values, and in becoming more visible, you unleash any hidden potential to genuinely effect change and make a valuable contribution across various spheres – personal, professional, societal, environmental and global. You already have all the tools you need to make a meaningful impact right now. Simply knowing that you've contributed in some way, leaving the world in a better place, will bring a sense of great fulfilment throughout life.

Contribution is about enriching the lives of others. It's the meaningful legacy you create beyond yourself and which surpasses any financial success you achieve in your lifetime. Being the catalyst for positive ripple effects, how you influence, inspire and impact the lives of others today is how you make your ultimate contribution to the world.

However, while you may never grasp the full extent of your impact, just know that your actions are creating positive ripple effects and this contribution is your gift to the world. In return, you receive the gift of growth. In 'Your Authentic Path', FOW 229, master coach Kate Trafford explained, 'As you strive to contribute, you grow as a person. The more you grow, the more you contribute. The more you contribute, the more you grow. It's like a virtuous, upward spiral of insight, self-discovery and opportunity.'

Your impact may not always be apparent through what you say, but rather could be through your purposeful listening, as silence can be how you make your powerful contribution. In my roles as podcast host and coach, attentive listening is essential. Remaining silent without interrupting, I focus on the speaker's words and non-verbal cues, which provides deeper connection and richer insights. Intentionally pausing before responding allows the speaker to express themselves fully. Moments of silence elevate the conversation, providing opportunities to delve deeper.

Also, never underestimate the significance of listening to your intuition and trusting it. Intuition is a highly developed system that rapidly processes information to guide incisive decision making to avoid potential harm. There may be times when you lack evidence to support this intuition and, on 2 October 2021, I encountered exactly what cognitive scientist Guy Claxton (1998) described as 'knowing without knowing why'.

One of my greatest joys in life is standing on the touchline as a proud mum watching Eddie skilfully playing rugby. After a closely contested match, his school team emerged victorious, prompting a celebratory team photo and joyous singing in the changing room. However, within the hour, Eddie complained of a headache and began vomiting. He has a high threshold for pain, but we recognised that this was different. Jon and I took him straight to hospital, but with Covid-19 restrictions still in place, only one of us could accompany him. After an initial assessment, his presentation wasn't deemed serious. However, I intuitively sensed an intense urgency to act and insisted on an immediate scan.

The scan revealed a fractured skull, ruptured artery and significant bleeding. Eddie was given morphine and promptly transferred to King's College Hospital. The neurosurgeon explained the necessary emergency surgery: a right temporal craniotomy and evacuation of the extradural hematoma. My absolute insistence had meant the bleed had been caught early. Deeply grateful to everyone involved in ensuring his swift recovery, 48 hours later Eddie returned home, swollen, bruised and exhausted. Trusting my 'knowing without knowing why' had contributed to saving Eddie's life.

It's not just about listening to your intuition about others' welfare, it's also about tuning into your own needs and desires. In FOW 180, 'Eliminating Stress', stress consultant Ruth Fogg explained how she works on the principle that 'everything starts somewhere' and added that, as most people hold stress in their bodies, it builds and builds until it manifests itself in physical illness as 'what the mind suppresses the body expresses'. Listening to your body's signals is essential.

As your time is stretched between roles as a parent, leader, family member, partner or friend, offering your undivided attention may be the most valuable gift you can give to others or to yourself. In fact, listening could be your greatest contribution.

George's Scrapbook
9 April 1944 – 25 March 1945

On 23 March 1944, in planning for his future, George entrusted Amie with securing him a country cottage to live in after the war, listing specific preferences and proposing desirable locations.

9 April 1944
On Destiny

Who am I, you may ask, a prisoner throughout this period to global warfare, immune, as I trust, from violent death, – who am I to discuss the workings of destiny, I who am least likely to show any of its effects, except perhaps in the greying of my hair as the years pour past; certainly, my claim to speak of destiny is no stronger than the next man's – another prisoner, of course – and a good deal weaker than yours.

For your house is likely to fall about your ears any moment now, but here in the heart of Germany, its rural, wooded heart, all is quiet and peaceful, and will be so until our rulers decide that war is now 'beyond a joke' and 'no laughing matter', that it has at last 'overstepped the mark', and 'exhausted its usefulness', that we have 'had suffering enough', that 'our young men have paid a great enough price'.

There now. And now I must speak of Destiny. But you do see, don't you, what my qualifications are?

We had been dusting around the room and this had come to light. A Bible. It fell open on the table, and at once we thought of the Virgilian lots and doing a Ouija and monkeying about with Delphic oracles and so on… I'm telling you this because, well, it may have some dramatically ironic interest should it be found some years hence, or should all of us be found here in 1973, still in captivity. Then you'd know, you see, how we got what we deserved. Me, I don't know, and it's still 1944. As I say, the Bible fell open at Leviticus, chapter 26. And we leant over and read at verse 38 – 'And ye shall

144

perish among the heathen, and the land of your enemies shall eat you up.'

You see? That fixed us, didn't it? Not bad, eh? Ominous, portentous, hideous; too terrible a warning possibly to have truth in it. Why not? Why? Why not? It might happen tomorrow, and that would be short enough notice in all conscience. We were, all of us, suitably impressed. Honestly, it did open there. I wouldn't say it if it weren't true, because the penalty for that might be even more unpleasant. I'm only writing this out just to show you the kind of thing we played at in '44.

Of course, I had a shot too, for the fun of the thing; opened the Bible, stubbed it and got caught up in Proverbs 6:10 'Yet a little sleep, a little slumber, a little folding of the hands to sleep.' Well, I ask you! That ain't prophecy, it's key-hole stuff! And I knew they'd all laugh like the devil, because, oh I freely admit it, I have spent most of my prison life on my bed, not sleeping I swear, thinking sometimes, sometimes reading, but not sleeping. And now it is '44 and I am in Germany, and alive. And I have written this down just in case you should find me in '45 asleep or, of course, eaten up!

8 June 1944

On James' 1st birthday *[George's nephew]* **and the invasion of Europe two days ago.** *[The Allies' D-Day landings on the beaches of Normandy]*

I was writing the last pages of Act I of 'Devil a bit of it' when the rumour reached our room. Thirty seconds later it was repeated by another messenger. A third arrived in five minutes with another rumour, this one that the first was true!

Finishing the Act was difficult, and I haven't been able, since then, to set my thoughts in order about Acts II and III.

I am waiting for the German papers and for news, and trying desperately to finish off the play. But it gets more and more melo-dramatic, and I want to kill everyone off, and then revive them and finish it so. But because it is essentially a piece 'to specification', my heart isn't wholly in it. My heart is in nothing but the invasion.

How does one express oneself in the event of an invasion? By taking part of course, defending or attacking, establishing or destroying bridge-heads. But the non-combatants – wives, mothers, children? By a deep and personal life-and-death connection with it.

But the prisoners, the soldiers of '39 who have no more brothers to lose, and no friends, how are they to express themselves? What do they wish to express? Joy at the sudden glimpse of future release, wonder at the unity of purpose, pride in the grim singleness of mind, shame in its grim ruthlessness, catharsis at the sight of the giant's fall. But how to express it? In verse, in drama, in music, in watercolour? In shouts of joy, in conviviality, sodality? With a slap on the back – or a diary entry?

James will never remember this first year of his life.

9 June 1944

I dropped a stone on the ant as it crossed the path. Listlessly sitting in the rain, I could think of nothing, think of doing nothing, do nothing. I saw the ant and the stone, and I thought 'This fact of life – and death. Let me prove it to myself yet again, I who have seen my mother, pale and peaceful in death, my grandfather small and wasted, my uncle, my dog, I who have heard of my father's losing struggle with death, of my brother's silent, anonymous death. Let me, once more, show it to be a mystery, strange, insoluble, final.'

And I dropped the stone. The ant was killed. I saw it squashed to the path, and I saw the stain of its life in the dust. Then I looked up, puzzled yet again by this strange finality, this irrevocable change from life into not life. I looked down to my proof but there was none. The body no longer lay there; the stain had gone. I had remembered the spot, could not forget it so soon.

As I looked, an ant completed its traverse of the path, and disappeared into the tall grasses. The same ant? How could I know?

A further mystery then? The mystery of re-birth? Or only of dissimulation, of protective colouring, natural camouflage, of survival of the fittest, of species and selection, habit and tooth and claw? All this and yet – Or was it not all this and moreover – I never saw my brother in death. Then – ?

A letter dated 28 September 1944 informs George of Amie's purchase: a charming 18th-century thatched cottage in a Buckinghamshire village, complete with fruit trees and jasmine framing the front door.

In November 1944, George received his certificate for passing the Intermediate Examination in Arts while held in Oflag VII B. He would continue to study throughout his life. In 1974, he completed a BA Honours degree from the Open University. In 1995, he was awarded honorary life membership by the Open University Shakespeare Society in recognition of his outstanding work.

George's regular scrapbook entries conclude here, transitioning from his personal collection of thoughts, letters and literary extracts to a comprehensive reflection of time spent in captivity. Detailing the living conditions and how they learned tolerance, he adopts a different writing style with a broader audience in mind.

25 March 1945
In the Enemy's Camp
A prisoner is a tangle of complicated emotions. It is not easy to explain him to a free-man, however sympathetic. There is much that must first be told before the prisoner can emerge as a comprehensible human being, matters of fact and routine, parole walks and perimeters for example, more subtle questions, too, of psychology and of character, prince of these, perhaps, being the prisoner's morbid desire to be 'understood'.

The real life of the prison, the intimate, sordid fellowship of the bedroom and the queue and the perimeter walk was anything but tedious. It was stimulating and pathetic and brutish. It was hysterically funny, and terrifying, and drab. It was commonplace, and it was unique. And it was all these things in the same half hour. But it was not tedious.

On our first day in a permanent prison, they issued us with a bunk, a blanket, mattress and pillow, knife, fork, spoon, bowl and mug – taking from us in return our British Army equipment and the last indignity, our hair. In addition to these German issues we had our own personal property – what we had brought with us through France, Belgium, Holland and Germany. Pitiful little bundles for the most part; and we dropped them at last, took off our boots, and lay down gratefully on our bunks.

A Single Room – with 30 Beds

For the prisoner, his bed was his castle. He felt that nothing could touch him there. Throughout the long years ahead of us, we were to know no greater security than this, to be lying upon our bed with our small possessions gathered around us. Of course, our kit had multiplied itself many times in those years. We had received clothes from home every quarter, and moreover, because we were always so close to penury, we had become frugal; we discarded nothing, for we never knew when it might come in useful.

We lived in rooms which were to serve us as dining room, bedroom, withdrawing room, kitchen, study, workshop, scullery, cellar and attic, coal shed and cloister. I can make the fact of over-crowding most vivid for you if I compare these rooms with some you know of in England: thus, a garage built to take two cars, nose to tail would be large enough to accommodate 12–15 officers, but this was at Eichstätt in '45, a civilised period by comparison with early days, when a room the size of a large drawing room held 27–30, and one with a floor area roughly that of a small suburban front lawn – anything from 60–105, depending on whether 2 or 3 tier bunks were used.

These bedrooms, then, were furnished simply. The bunks lined the four walls, and jutted out from them at right angles to form barriers splitting the room up into several little compartments. In each of these was a small kitchen table with plain, backless stools ranged around it, one for each officer, and here, eight or more of us would sit down to eat. Tall lockers were dotted around the room, making passageways through it and flanking the bedsides. It was on these lockers that we pinned up our photographs, and slung our rough-hewn bookshelves.

We had a stove in the centre of the room, and several examples of the invention called, inappropriately enough, the 'smokeless heater', and as one of these was in use at every hour of the day, the fumes from it rose to the ceiling, discoloured the plaster walls and brought tears to our eyes and choked us as we worked the hellish machines.

We might wait for three years before discovering that mahjong pieces could be pierced and sewn on as buttons, or that an old pair of trousers could be cut up and used as powerful straps for a pack, toothbrushes as knitting needles, and mattresses as artist's canvasses. In time every article declared its secondary function to us, and we withdrew it from the obscurity of some dusty cardboard box, congratulating ourselves on our forethought and thrift. We could not find it in our hearts to say of a thing that it was a dead loss. Something could always be saved, we were sure of that. So sure we came to look beyond the obvious functions of an object in search of one less apparent. We used fruit jellies for printing off maps, boot polish as fuel, and once, in emergency, bread and blancmange powder as medium in which to model a dummy prisoner!

We became so attached to our junk that whenever we changed camp we could not bear to part with it. It was packed up carefully and duly searched, both on leaving one camp and on arrival at the next. We had no shame. We displayed the trash and saw it through those terrible searches and, after unpacking it lovingly at the other end, surrounded ourselves again with some old curling photographs, a ditty-box, a book or two, a comb, an empty tin, bared our feet and lay down on our beds, in our new home.

Life of Captivity

We have seen the surrender of the soldier, and the prisoner being led away to his cell. We have looked at his cell and seen him lying on his bunk there, reading or gazing up at the ceiling. What is he thinking about? Is he planning an escape, or day-dreaming of home or beauty, or of steak and kidney pie? At any moment the German bugle may sound, and he will be dragged on to parade to be counted. At any moment news may come of a truck load of parcels having been despatched from Geneva. At any moment – nothing may happen at all, and he will spend the entire day on his bed there. 'Yes,' you will say, 'but what kind of a day?' We shall see...

The prisoner was by no means an early riser. No, the prisoner was little inclined to leave the shelter of his bed, particularly for the tedious ceremony of morning-appel – and this on an empty stomach, for generally we broke our fast after the parade, in order to fill in the morning somehow – with this thin slice of rye bread.

As the years sauntered by and we amassed more and more baggage, every corner of the room became littered with the odds and ends one would expect to find in the toolshed or at the far end of the garage. Beneath the beds there were battered suitcases, cigarette ends and rows of dirty boots and shoes; on the lockers, cardboard boxes piled one atop the other, kit bags and oddly shaped bundles, books and papers and empty tins, and over all a two-inch blanket of dust; more clothing on the beds, more boxes, and a cigarette packet; and on the table, some potato peelings, a broken tin opener, and a tin mug with the enamel cracked and flaking off.

These were our living conditions. We were overcrowded, badly equipped, ill lit at night time, necessitous always. What we lacked we were forced to improvise, so that there was in the early days no peace in the rooms, but the continual banging, thumping and shouting of the carpenter and the tin-smith, and the constant passage of heavy feet. Such a life would not have been possible for long. We therefore adapted ourselves to our environment, instituted a two-hour silence period in the afternoons, and learned to speak in a low murmur that would not irritate or distract.

In these rooms we learned tolerance and patience, for we discovered that there was nothing to be gained by an outburst of temper. Each man got on the nerves of his companion; but they were to be companions for many months yet, and we decided it were better to cut our losses than our throats. Each man had his private worries and sorrows with which only he could deal. But we all had the one great fact of exile in common and this we could make easier for all only by suppression of the more violent emotions, in an attempt to live, if not in amity, at any rate in peace and quiet.

What shaped the prisoner's life and what mattered to him was not the international wrangling but the number of slices of bread he could have for breakfast, and what likelihood there was of his getting back home again this year sometime, or next year, indeed ever. These private doubts and fears made up the prisoner's complex emotional history, made up his day of boredom, and hunger, and wretchedness, relieved as it was by occasional comedy, occasional meals, occasional good news…

'Freiheit und Brot' *[freedom and bread]*
'Freiheit und Brot' were the two great factors that determined the course of our day. Our prison existence was a long struggle for both, but whereas we became reconciled to the loss of freedom, we could never in all that term effect a compromise with hunger. We were under-nourished throughout, and we could not put the thought aside. Food became an obsession with us.

The Geneva Convention laid down that we should receive from the Germans the same rations as their own back line garrison troops. But the Germans were engaged upon Total War – and they worked to an intricate scheme of rationing by which the Reich was divided up into innumerable categories with varying claims upon the food stores of Germany, the lowest category being Prisoners of War.

The Red Cross determined on a policy of supplying each

151

prisoner with one parcel a week. Now, because German rations were smaller than had been catered for, and the German advance something larger, it became increasingly difficult to get the parcels through to Switzerland and then into Germany and when they did arrive at the camps they had to supplant, not merely supplement, the local food supply. This then was for us the major question of the war – the arrival or non-arrival of our parcels. Upon the answer to that depended all our enterprises and pastimes.

Contribute: Reflections with Actions

⬈ Your Greatest Gift

Listening may seem simple but it's not always easy. Resist the urge to respond, give opinions, lecture, or offer advice. Just listen. Don't forget to listen to yourself as well. Reflect on your self-care practices and how they align with your purposeful journey. Identify areas where you could make improvements. Relationships thrive on time, effort, love and attention. Your investment in them is reciprocated, yielding immeasurable rewards. They shape your experiences, and without them, the world feels lonely. Contribute your gift of presence.

⬈ What Really Matters

Imagine describing the world to a stranger, devoid of any knowledge. What aspects would you include, and what would you omit? Take a moment to reflect in your journal on this hypothetical conversation. It's a revealing exercise that unveils what truly holds significance in your life.

⬈ Positive Impacts

How can you make a positive impact on others and contribute to causes, charities or communities aligned with your purpose? Consider performing random acts of kindness, recycling for sustainability, volunteering, mentoring, sharing your knowledge, paying it forward, expressing gratitude or giving back. Reflect on the personal fulfilment derived from your contributions and how they may create further positive ripples.

Contribute: Celebrate and Continue

↗ TAP INTO THE TINGLE

I've noticed that discussing the why often elicits the primal response of goosebumps, signalling personal and meaningful experiences of inspiration, connection, awe, joy, pride, nostalgia or excitement. Celebrate these goosebumps, as they indicate authentic significance and next time they occur, 'tap into the tingle' to explore the source of your emotions further.

Step 8: Contribute – Summary

Your perspective shapes your contribution, enabling you to make a meaningful impact. Purpose goes beyond just yourself, prompting you to consider how you can focus your contribution personally, professionally or both. Every moment offers the opportunity to contribute uniquely.

Step 9: Change

Change with your evolving purpose: embrace growth and transformation at every stage of life.

In January 2024, Jon and I visited Robben Island prison, South Africa. Our guide was a softly spoken, elderly former prisoner called Vuyani. Arrested, convicted and imprisoned for five years for sabotage in 1976, he shared his humbling experience of the hardship and conditions that he and other prisoners had endured. As I stood outside Nelson Mandela's cell, or the 'Presidential Suite', as Vuyani named it, I tried to imagine Mandela reflecting on the plan he would focus on once freed.

Stepping back onto the pontoon in Cape Town harbour, I realised that this was likely where Mandela took his first steps of freedom, ready to activate his purpose-driven plan to build a united country. While Mandela's impact is undeniable, with his purpose to ensure that this chapter of apartheid history is not forgotten, it was Vuyani whose experiences and words are now etched onto my soul.

If you ever find yourself admiring individuals you wish to emulate, just as I had revered George as a writer, remember that their journey likely started from much humbler beginnings and evolved over time to reach the current level of success that you now see. By understanding how the external world mirrors your internal landscape of thoughts, beliefs and intentions, you become aware of your ability to initiate change, both within yourself and in the world. You hold the power to enact change, but it requires your conscious choice to do so.

In FOW 109, 'Science of Why', Pieter Kruger emphasised the importance of having a plan and a purpose, as sustainable behavioural change occurs when individuals understand the why behind their actions, reinforcing that 'ultimately, it's all about the why'. Incorporating a meaningful why and purpose into all your activities, having a plan with values-based, purpose-driven intentions and focusing on them daily isn't just a recommendation, it's essential.

Purpose in life is now recognised as a central component of determining quality of life and positive wellbeing, supported by a growing body of research showing its correlation with numerous benefits such as increased vitality (Giannis et al 2023), improved sleep (Kim et al 2015), mental health (Kang et al 2021), wellbeing (Friedman et al 2007) and reduced risk of mortality (Boyle et al 2009; Alimujiang et al 2019). Dan Buettner (2020) identified the key elements linked to longevity and happiness and in his *Live to 100: Secrets of the Blue Zones* documentary series, he said that 'the same things that help us live a long, healthy life are the things that make life worth living'.

Greater purpose in life has also been associated with a reduced risk of Alzheimer's disease (Boyle et al 2009), is seen to lessen the burden following stroke (Kim et al 2015), chronic pain and frailty (Gale et al 2014), whereas reduced life satisfaction has been correlated with the development of chronic diseases (Feller et al 2013). Scientific research continues to explore what benefits purpose in life has for health and wellbeing. In the meantime, without any drawbacks I see adopting a more purposeful 'Way of Life' as a logical choice.

Holding a doctorate in cognitive neuroscience specialising in the unconscious processing of emotion and behavioural change, Dr Lynda Shaw (FOW 230, 'Recalibrate Your Thinking') has always been curious to understand why people behave as they do. Lynda explained that 'our brain changes our behaviour and our behaviour changes our brain. It's this glorious feedback loop that we're able to manage very well, when we're aware of how to do it.'

Lynda reassuringly stated that we're more in control of our brains than we think, but not all of the time because that wouldn't be helpful in certain situations. However, ultimately we're able to dictate our brains' actions some of the time and on purpose. Change, then, not only becomes achievable but manageable. Therefore, your daily behaviour and habits hold considerable influence, shaping your future to work for or against you. Even the smallest, imperceptible changes compound over time, so it's essential to assess your habits and align them with your values-based intentions.

In a separate conversation, Lynda explained to me how to have and keep a healthy brain. Other than sharing the more obvious benefits of sleep, nutrition, rest, play, exercise, stress reduction and work, Lynda suggested that a key ingredient that can make the most difference to your physical and mental health is… purpose.

Lynda proposed that the pursuit of happiness can be misleading, suggesting instead that happiness may be a side effect of purpose. Breaking this down from her neuroscience perspective, she explained that when stressed, your focus narrows to tackle the perceived threat activating the body's in-built security system, which is always on high alert. However, as these perceived threats aren't actually life threatening, over-focusing on non-essential matters impedes your creativity and compromises your brain health.

When you focus your attention on something outside yourself, such as your purpose, a variety of neurochemicals are released. Acting with purpose stimulates the release of dopamine, generating a sense of reward or anticipation of reward. Altruistic deeds prompt the release of nitric oxide, while increased happiness triggers serotonin release. Involvement in social groups triggers oxytocin and feeling energised leads to endorphin release.

Recognising how purposeful action can trigger positive neurochemical responses highlights how purpose forms the basis of your happiness. Instead of pursuing happiness in life, focus on purposeful activities in both life and work, as happiness naturally ensues. Similarly, when you prioritise contribution over achievement, success often emerges naturally.

Remaining laser focused on what aligns with your values and channelling your energy towards fulfilment can drive meaningful changes in your work. While multitasking may appear productive, in reality it often leads to rapid task switching (Lahnakoski et al 2017), sacrificing time, efficiency and ultimately, profit for businesses. Maintain focus to enhance productivity and make more significant progress towards your intentions.

Despite recognising change is essential and being open to making necessary adjustments, are you still struggling or experiencing resistance? Possible causes might include fear, indecision, uncertainty, lack of knowledge or unfamiliarity.

International negotiator Derek Arden (FOW 192, 'Everything is Negotiable') believes change is necessary, saying, 'If you always do what you've always done, you'll always get what you've always got. So go out and try something different. The world is moving so quickly. It's really exciting to be alive at this time in the development of the world but keep doing things differently. Go out and help other people and have some fun. Life is not a rehearsal.' Indeed, it isn't. This is your one and only life, yet I still see so many people living as though they have a spare in reserve. Today is your life. Embrace every moment and build habits that bring you joy. How will you choose to spend your time? Remember, there's a vast difference between filling in the moments and creating fulfilling moments.

Your responsibility extends beyond your lifetime, encompassing the passing on of knowledge to peers and future generations. Your experiences, including both successes and failures, serve as valuable lessons for others and become your legacy. Don't allow your knowledge to remain buried in your head. This concept echoes notes made in George's scrapbook from John Lyly's play *Campaspe* in January 1943, justifying his focus on study over fighting: 'It is better to have in your court a wise man, than in your ground a golden mine. Therefore would I leave war to study wisdom, were I Alexander.'

Access to knowledge is invaluable, but it also poses a problem as it can become overwhelming and time consuming. Amassing information instead of taking action causes useful knowledge to dissipate before it's applied. That's why I emphasise the practice of Reflection with Action across all nine steps. The issue preventing you from achieving what you desire in life isn't always a lack of knowledge but rather a lack of action. Be mindful of balancing knowledge acquisition with taking action to achieve your purposeful intentions.

March 2020 now feels like a distant memory. While one of my business ventures abruptly ended, numerous new opportunities emerged. Within the same month, I attended my first Professional Speaking Association meeting, and launched a coaching business and podcast. What initially seemed like a daunting learning curve turned out to be a series of midlife beginnings, opportunities to leverage all my past experiences.

As I entered my grandmother's home after her funeral in 2022, I paused at the hallway mirror, a silent witness to decades of memories spent with Ruth and George. In the reflection, I saw all the evolving roles I've played across my lifetime, each revealing 'every circumstance of life, every facet of living', a testament to the person I've become. Embracing change, being open minded and having a strong sense of purpose, I now recognise, more than ever, my responsibility to continually evolve as change is the only constant.

George's Scrapbook
15 April 1945 – 23 April 1945

Change is inevitable. During his lifetime, George witnessed significant transformations both within himself and in the world around him. Recognising the need to evolve, he dedicated himself to continuous growth. Despite the challenges of captivity, he'd spent each day writing, studying and reading, accumulating a wealth of knowledge and wisdom. Taking decisive action, he'd then applied this wisdom to navigate life's journey.

Found separate from his scrapbook, these final notes were hastily written in pencil on loose sheets of paper marking his final days as a POW.

15 April 1945 *[George's 27th birthday]*
Curlew or plover or peewit at 4am in the morning.

16 April 1945
During that trouble of the 14th, it was difficult to think of anything. I was face down in the ditch for, I suppose, 20 minutes, forced to lie there passively while the US planes swept up and down over and across the road backwards and forwards.

After years of captivity and just as the war was ending, on 14 April 1945, many of George's fellow British POW officers were tragically killed or injured by low-flying Allied aircraft as they were marched out of the camp. Mistaken for enemy troops, 14 British officers were killed, 46 wounded. Recounting his ordeal to my father many years later, George described it as the most terrifying experience of his life.

My first thought was – thank goodness, now I have a reasonable excuse for jettisoning my heavy pack. I had been worried lest it should appear ignominious to junk it. However I had carried it for 15 minutes, the stitches had held.

After that, when the gunning became continuous and systematic (there is a plane very low now) I knew I must think of (many planes low) something – and how to, what shall I think of – but it's different now, for me I have my writing – (gone again).

Well, I thought of thinking about God, but I'd had some setback there – so not religion – that couldn't help me. Therefore there was nothing for me to think about except myself. I was living now but I might be dead in about 1/1,000 seconds, so what could be done?

I buried my face as each wave came, closed my eyes, held my breath and then granted its release like tensing myself against the dentist's probe. It was like a dentist's drill along that road – I never looked to see whence they came or how many or their routine. I was in too exposed a position to give myself any hope of dispassionate observation. It seemed unlikely I should survive. But later, when I found myself still untouched, I found I became preoccupied with the hope of survival – assuming it would happen. So I superstitiously banished that too prominent wish, lest it should damage my chances.

What remained? Myself and my hopes. At each sweep I artificially induced pictures of Amie and Boy, the cottage, and myself writing; repeated to myself – the cottage and myself writing – that was my faith.

And now the danger is from bombing. Thank God we walk by night. By day there is absolutely no peace. Poor devils of civilians everywhere. It needed this to remind us of the terror and the brutality of the thing. Not under any circumstances should the thing be allowed or continued.

Oh, the ice is breaking up on every side.

By the way, things noticed during that gunning, the dank of the grass beneath my face, criss-crossed with shafts of light, like a tiny cathedral. Life does this, the macrocosm is violently crumbling to pieces and of the pieces are formed perfect and immaculate microcosm. Nothing dies – and there are no absolutes! Everything relates to something.

> Immediately after the last sweep, silence and the gentle cleansing of the air by the lark's syringe of song.

Despite his circumstances, encompassing both terror and beauty, emphasising the unity of all beings, George still writes.

> **17 April 1945**
> We crossed the Danube at two this morning. A broad canal-like length of water (Ernsgaden on the Danube). We were not ordinarily early risers. But convention clung hard to most of us and we would shave each day, wash – say – twice a day and bathe as often as once every three weeks. But this latter was not due so much to slovenliness as to the German hygienic provision.
> In emergency – that is to say at a time when everything is stripped from us, all our poses, illusion and whims, leaving simply the fact of self in emergency, then one searches to supplement this one bleak fact.

> **18 April 1945**
> Immersed as we now are in rural scenes of life, it is difficult for us to imagine a fitter place to be told of the war's end. It is typical of these last few days of near destruction and of men and women and children dying by their thousands in half an hour in Wurzburg that a gosling should be born before our eyes. So it goes on. So life renews itself and the cycle proceeds.

George's affection for birds has shone throughout bringing him much joy and uplifting his spirits in dark times: the stork, ducks, blackbird, linnet, lark, curlew, plover and peewit all mentioned. Here, while resting briefly in a barn, he records the wonder of a gosling's birth even capturing the scene in a hurried pencil sketch.

We are reduced in kit and morale to the bare essentials – bully and bravado – stoicism and corned beef, nothing else matters. I long for my own farm life, my quiet cottage, like these here with their fruit trees and hops.

Food for the mind and food for the body, Stoicism is considered just as essential as food.

Lovely weather for life. That's what we believe in – Life – our own life. I should like Peace to come to the world for the world is ready for it. I forgive and forget the injuries inflicted. There is no war guilt. No one man could have conceived such a disaster. Tolerance.

Always one to find a positive spin, he'd even say 'lovely weather for ducks' when it rained!

23 April 1945
A week later. It has not been possible to think or write or read or draw – seriously. I have been able only to scribble and sketch and gossip with myself and my neighbours. We are all jumpy. Witness the speed with which we raced through to Mainburg – streaks in the sky or an alarm blowing.

> Planes, planes looking for us –
> looking to save or to slay us.
> Now the technique is to use the
> white flag – after the emergency.
> Now the technique is to act the
> civilian, the refugee, the 'Kriegie'.

This is to return by easy stages. This barn and farm nomadic life is to soften the possibly too wonderful peace of Peace.
And after? Resist and denounce retaliation and all unfriendliness.

163

George made a conscious decision to release resentment towards his captors, recognising that holding onto negative emotions would only prolong his imprisonment. Unable to alter the past, as a pacifist he focused on embracing forgiveness and finding peace. Upon release from the camp, George became aware of the scale of the atrocities that had taken place elsewhere during WW2. His last significant action was to attend the Nuremberg Trials, as he said he'd wanted to 'see their faces'.

With this symbolic closure, he began his new 'Way of Life'.

Change: Reflections with Actions

➤ GIFT OF FORGIVENESS

Are you holding yourself prisoner right now? Forgiveness liberates you from the past, empowering you to live with purpose. Take control of your life by releasing any resentment and managing your feelings. Who or what do you need to forgive today? Focus on forgiveness to move forward with purpose, creating space for rejuvenation, reflection and self-renewal.

➤ TRANSFORMATIVE STEPS

Transformation comes from change. Reflect on your past experiences of successfully navigating and embracing change. What fears, resistance or limitations did you manage to overcome? Extract the lessons to apply to your desired transformations. Choose an area for change and take one small step each day towards achieving it, starting today.

➤ LIFE PURPOSE RULES

Welcome change as a catalyst for personal growth and a purpose-driven life. Picture your ideal self, embodying any desired changes you wish to make. Identify the specific actions and attitudes that define this version of you. Integrate these qualities into your daily life, forming purposeful rules to live by. Establish a feedback loop to regularly evaluate your progress, adjusting actions and strategies accordingly.

Change: Celebrate and Continue

➤ FRIENDSHIP

Life may throw you curveballs, but your friendships will carry you through them. Together you become stronger. With friendship, anything is possible. Reflect on how maintaining relationships provide support and purpose in your life. Who really matters to you? Celebrate your friendships and focus on any that require your attention.

Step 9: Change – Summary

Creating a life of purpose requires dedication and perseverance. To lead an extraordinary life, you must be willing to step out of your comfort zone prepared to explore what paradigm shifts need to occur embracing change through taking meaningful action. Activate your vision, mission and purpose. Your life's work isn't achieved in a day; it simply requires you to start, plan and then focus.

Part 3: Focus – Summary

Creating something valuable takes time, patience, knowledge, consistent effort and a positive attitude. It's about taking action every day. Action drives change. Who you become is your choice. You alone are responsible for your transformation and your transitions. Your focus shapes your path, so why settle for a life devoid of joy and fulfilment when you have the power to create a Focus on Why 'Way of Life' filled with purpose and meaning?

Change can be unsettling, as it leads to the unknown. However, it's crucial to embrace change as a catalyst for growth. Adapt to evolving circumstances and seize opportunities for learning, growth and transformation. As you evolve, so will your purpose to reflect this ongoing journey of personal growth and fulfilment. Translate knowledge into action by reflecting on your circumstances and determining actionable steps within your control. This brings you right back to Step 1: Control.

Whether by choice or external circumstances, every shift in direction or transition is an opportunity to reset and realign your purpose. With the Focus on Why Framework, you can adapt or develop a new plan to navigate these changes effectively. Remember, starting anew doesn't mean discarding what you've learned or accomplished; it's about combining all your resources, experiences and strengths.

Conclusion

Imperfection

In what would become some of his final reflections in life, George wrote of how he saw 'glimpses of small perfections' in his own work, claiming only to come near 'once or twice, no more'. With George no longer here to articulate his intentions and knowing what a skilled writer he was with high standards, I acknowledge the possibility of there being entries or poems he may have preferred to have remained private and unpublished. Despite this, I view my selection of his content as integral to understanding the evolution of his purpose as it captures his journey of self-discovery, showcasing his imperfections and growth as he navigated and explored the person he was becoming.

Motivated by various factors, perfection is often seen as the standard you strive to achieve for happiness and fulfilment. When driven by fear of failure, comparison, low self-esteem or the desire to avoid criticism, falling short of these standards can lead to feelings of disappointment, inadequacy or resentment, resulting in self-criticism, anxiety and procrastination. However, when pursued for growth, perfection can provide a sense of focus and act as a tool for problem-solving, with your progress celebrated through self-compassion.

For decades, I'd attached my self-worth to meeting unrealistic standards I'd set myself to attain. It took me years to realise that my pursuit of perfection, fuelled by a mindset rooted in comparison and fearing shame and vulnerability, was ultimately an illusion – unattainable and devoid of value. Recognising its futility, I embraced my uniqueness and imperfections, prioritising self-improvement and growth, which proved to be far more sustainable, meaningful and fulfilling.

It's important to recognise that making mistakes and experiencing failure is a natural part of being human. The issue doesn't just lie in striving for perfection but also in undervaluing your imperfections and the valuable lessons they offer. Sharing these imperfections can open you up to support and connection with others. Taking responsibility for and embracing your imperfections is a profound act of self-worth and self-acceptance.

When courage meets imperfection, it grants you permission to simply be yourself, free from pretence or self-doubt; no facades, impostor phenomenon or armour – just you. Your imperfections won't hinder your pursuit of intentions or purpose; rather they allow you to fully embrace who you are. Living authentically matters. It involves being true to yourself, understanding your motivations and living on your own terms. Ensure your path is genuinely yours, not what others expect. Ultimately it's about choice – you decide what you think, how you feel and how you respond in every situation. Believing in your actions and their purpose matters. Living with purpose means pursuing something greater than yourself while staying true to who you are.

A true life involves showing vulnerability and social courage, even in the face of adversity. Authenticity requires having the courage of your own convictions and standing up for your values, as demonstrated in our narratives, George, aged 22–27 and myself, today aged 49. Throughout our existential quests for meaning, you've witnessed how relationships and bonds sustained us through hardship, observed our commitment to continuous self-improvement through introspection and seen how to align actions and intentions with life purpose and values. As we navigated changing circumstances, we applied grit, resilience and adaptability, liberated our minds through enhanced creativity and reflection, appreciated the world's beauty and ascribed meaning to daily events. Applying lessons learned through conscious choice, acceptance and exploration of our passions we've created impactful and enduring ripple effects.

The lessons to apply from this book are yours to choose, as what holds significance for you may differ from our perspectives. You alone have the responsibility to sculpt your purposeful life and create an intentional living legacy. Enjoy your journey and live it fully!

Bridging the Gap

In my teenage years, I had a brilliant rowing coach who guided me to become a national rowing champion in 1990, despite dramatically capsizing my boat the previous year. Coaches were mostly absent in my twenties and thirties, but it was in my forties that various coaches and mentors significantly enhanced my personal and professional growth. I shifted from feeling frustrated and unfulfilled with my life to believing I could achieve my full potential, change direction to pursue my passions and leverage my strengths and talents to craft the authentic, purposeful life I desired.

You could spend your entire life feeling unfulfilled, focusing more on what you don't want rather than what you do. However, this need not be your fate – it's a choice. Recognising that there's a gap between your current situation and your future vision is crucial. Coaching bridges that gap. Through a reflective, creative and collaborative process, coaching illuminates what you really want, need and value, facilitating a transformational journey from where you are to where you want to be. Have you identified any gaps in your life?

Working with a coach helps you to clarify thoughts, beliefs and desires, become more self-aware, align your actions with your values, focus on what's blocking you and shift your perspective to unlock your potential for fulfilment across all areas of life and work.

Through my coaching experiences, both as recipient and provider, coupled with ongoing training to enhance my coaching skills, I've witnessed profound, transformative shifts in perspective. These shifts have brought various benefits, such as aligning values with purpose, increasing self-awareness and self-esteem, overcoming perceived limitations, embracing new paths and integrating regular reflection into actionable steps.

Just like purpose, personal development is a lifelong journey that demands continuous commitment, application and effort. I've invested in diverse forms of self-improvement – books, courses, mentoring and coaching – to encourage my ongoing growth and evolution. This journey of mastery has brought me deep and profound understanding, enriching experiences and ongoing transformation, turning my life into an exhilarating and fulfilling adventure.

To determine whether coaching might benefit you, consider these questions:

- What are the three main challenges you're currently facing?
- What would happen if you were to overcome these challenges?
- What consequences might you face if your challenges remained unresolved?

When you prioritise values, purpose, fulfilment, joy, significance, contribution and collaboration, you transition from simply existing to living. This shift to flourishing is profound. Instead of passively sleep-walking through life, you're actively and consciously crafting a life that aligns with your aspirations.

From Beyond the Wire

Dreams and Schemes

So, what happened next for George? Having narrowly survived the strafing, while being repatriated on 8 May 1945 – VE Day – he faced yet another near-death experience. Awaiting his turn to board the plane, standing on the runway he witnessed the plane before his crash on take-off, resulting in the tragic loss of all on board.

Arriving back in England, he finally learned the fate of his brother, Donald. On 3 June 1941, aged 25, his Blenheim was shot down over the English Channel. His body was recovered by French locals and laid to rest in Plurien Communal Cemetery in Brittany. George visited the village and received an emotional welcome, with tables brought out into the square for a celebratory feast.

After attending the Nuremberg Trials and filming *The Captive Heart*, officially released from active military duty on 1 June 1946 with honorary rank of captain, he settled into Jasmine Cottage, the home Amie had found. There, he devoted several years to writing plays, articles and manuscripts, also working as a freelance radio writer for Radio-diffusion Française (RDF) in Paris between 1947 and 1948.

From another diary, George documents his days, some marked with success, others bad or hard when articles or manuscripts had been rejected. Maintaining his sardonic humour, he found pleasure in pasting all his rejection slips on the wall, even quipping that each is a 'very worthwhile souvenir, having significance, utility and also decorative value. It will be sad when I can paste no more, for editors' insistence on my merit.'

Undeterred by rejections, he persisted in pursuing his dreams, making plans to achieve a number of written stories and words within set timescales, tutoring pupils privately to subsidise his income. One day there was a knock on the front door of Jasmine Cottage. It was Ruth delivering a telegram on behalf of her parents who ran the village Post Office. Ruth and George married in June 1950, coinciding with George's first official appointment as a BBC staff playwright. Continuing with the 1990 interview, George shared how he'd got the position.

AMY: So when you came out of prison, where did you go and what did you do? Went back to your family?

GEORGE: Yeah, but when I finally came out I saw a job advertised in the BBC.

AMY: And you went straight for it?

GEORGE: I went for it. I had written in prison the play, which was an adaptation of a short story by Joseph Conrad. We were just going to produce it and put it on when the war finished. So I came back and rewrote it as a television play. Although I knew nothing about television, but then no one else did either. And sent it in. Then an advertisement appeared for a job and the head of drama at the BBC was Val Gielgud, John Gielgud's brother, and at the interview he said, 'Oh, you wrote *The Secret Sharer* by Conrad, didn't you? Adapted it? Yes, I like it very much. I want to put it on and would you like this job?' And I got the job.

AMY: Without even asking?

GEORGE: Well, I applied. I got the play and I got the job and I was one of the first staff writers on BBC Television.

RUTH: You wrote that in prison.

GEORGE: I wrote it in prison. Knowing nothing about television. What would you know about television in prison? It hadn't opened, reopened anyway.

RUTH: And that you now play golf with a guy who...

GEORGE: Yeah, I play golf, regular golf with a group we call the 'Old Goats' and one of them is a Welshman who was a pilot of Lancaster Bombers, and when they were all finished, they

sacrificed their VE leave in order to fly into Germany and
France and bring out the prisoners and he did that. So the
guy I'm playing golf with…

RUTH: He's crying now.

GEORGE: No, I'm not… is one of the guys who flew me out.

RUTH: He's a lovely man.

GEORGE: Anyway, there we are.

Having transformed captivity into an opportunity for growth and
flourishing, George's purpose had been to liberate his mind; his plan
had been to become a writer and he had remained focused on his
'dreams and schemes'. He'd completed his dramatisation of *The Secret
Sharer* ready for a performance in the camp. Understandably, their focus
had shifted away from amateur theatricals with the onset of the D-Day
landings in Normandy; however, his adaptation had safely made its way
back to England with George to play a crucial role in securing his first
full-time writing job.

He progressed to drama script supervisor, then, in 1955, transi-
tioned to another major TV production company, Associated British
Television (ABC TV), setting up the drama department and creating
Armchair Theatre as script editor. In *The Daily Telegraph* on 7 December
1955, George explained that 'the successful television play should have
a strong contemporary story plus a subplot, preferably of emotional
entanglement. The story should be classifiable as a study of the troubles
of the people next door, or, if the troubles are slightly unsavoury, of the
people next door but one. In telling the story, however, the television
writer will not be holding, as it were, the mirror up to nature. He should
be smearing nature on a slide.'

In 1957, along with Ruth and their three-year-old daughter
Catharine (my mother), George emigrated to Australia. For five years,
he lived and worked in Sydney as a radio and television playwright for
the Australian Broadcasting Commission (ABC) drama department. In
an interview for *The ABC Weekly* in 1958, George said, 'I had always
wanted to write, even at the risk of starving', and cited his major
influences, 'Dialogue from Coward, thought from Shaw, wit (if any)

from Wilde and humanity from Chekhov. The proper study of mankind is man. When I observe people, it isn't their surface motives that interest me, but their real motives, and when you've got those, you have a play.'

Nostalgic for the English lifestyle, they returned to England in 1962. George became head of drama for ABC TV in Teddington with a £1 million budget and staff of 200; he oversaw all drama productions. His focus on becoming a writer during those POW years had led him to living out a 'Way of Life' he'd desired. Essentially, George now found himself in the company of some of his early writing influences such as Noel Coward, who he met in a lavish Savoy Hotel suite to discuss the adaptation of a short story into a TV play. Enjoying one another's company so much, they ended up sitting on the settee singing together late into the evening with a butler serving them their drinks.

Remember how George had watched *The Wizard of Oz* three times in one afternoon before heading off to France in an attempt to escape his reality? Well perhaps life wasn't the 'painted fantasy' or the 'ridiculously optimistic' notion he'd once criticised the film for being, as two decades later George proved that the 'dreams you dare to dream really do come true'. To discuss a role he had in mind for Judy Garland, he visited her London home and after the interview, Judy played Liza Minnelli's first LP to him, proudly stating 'She's better than her mother!'

George's infectious enthusiasm for life made him a captivating storyteller, often becoming the centre of entertainment at parties. As he shared his wealth of knowledge and love for learning with everyone he encountered, his legacy flourished. I literally owe my life to the choices George made in captivity. Shouldering criticism from fellow soldiers for not attempting to escape, enduring hardships and trusting in the hope of freedom, he maintained faith in his purpose to become a writer. His daily decisions not only shaped his destiny but also mine.

His unwavering commitment to those decisions enabled me to fulfil two roles to create our collaborative living legacy 85 years apart: to become the 'later chronicler' who 'must speak of this' ensuring his Commonplace Scrapbook did 'contribute something to history'; and to evolve his 'Way of Life' proposal to highlight the power of a Focus on Why for future generations.

Writing remained George's lifelong passion and purpose, sustaining him for 50 years. When we laid him to rest, the most magnificent rainbow arched across the sky. Now every time I catch sight of one, it serves as a poignant reminder of George, perhaps also suggesting life is indeed filled with rainbows and lullabies.

The Great Escape

In 2009, I watched a BBC TV programme called *Monty Halls' Great Escape*. Turning his back on city life to rebuild a crofter's cottage on the west coast of Scotland, Monty embraced a humble lifestyle with his dog. I was so spellbound by this idyllic idea of escaping far from the bustle of modern life, Holly even checked to make sure I wasn't entertaining thoughts of uprooting our lives to pursue such a dream. Though I wasn't, it had planted a seed to escape to a more serene lifestyle in the future.

Over the next decade, my family's lifestyle underwent significant changes. In 2014, both Jon and I embarked on new jobs in London. By 2016, realising this lifestyle was not conducive to our health, I resigned. With my family, I spent that summer at my father's home in the Dordogne, reflecting on the importance of crafting a new 'Way of Life'. Amid this introspection, following a powerful electrical thunderstorm, I gained clarity on both our individual and collective aspirations. This marked a pivotal reset in our journey, allowing us to create our own atmosphere and our own way to escape.

With a clear vision for our new lifestyle, it took three years to establish the foundations for the new 'Way of Life' we now live and love. Since 2019, Jon's transition away from his city job has significantly improved his health and granted us the freedom to travel at our leisure. We prioritise our health, no longer drink alcohol and enjoy being Saturday 'parkrun tourists'. We continue to operate as a team just as we've done since 1995, supporting each other's endeavours, Jon now managing our property business while I focus on coaching, podcasting and writing. Our transformed lifestyle is a product of intentional, conscious design.

In 2019, I briefly met Monty after attending his talk on the elemental forces of success – vision, drive, resilience and belief. Stressing the importance of values being the still point in a turning world, Monty challenged the audience to reflect on the driving force and source of our pride – our identity – reminding us that possibilities are endless and that our limits are, like our fears, largely an illusion. Sharing the sentiment that attitude is the difference between an ordeal and an adventure, he emphasised that attitude is a choice.

In 2024, in FOW 409, 'Turn the Tide', Monty spoke of the importance of making conscious life choices, of your attitude, of resetting and of taking 'control of pretty much any situation' saying that 'there's always a way'. He described how the last ten years have been very turbulent, adding that 'all of us carry a mark from those times'. However, he also said, 'Don't underestimate the positive impact that has had on you. It has made us all more resilient, more flexible. We're tougher now than we were ten years ago.'

What is clear from all the stories I've shared and from this intertwined journey with my grandfather is the importance of remaining focused in pursuing our own purposeful 'dreams and schemes'. From beyond the wire and beyond the grave, George has left us with an inspirational lesson: each of us has the choice to plan our own great escape.

References

Series of Coincidences

Focus on WHY podcast: amyrowlinson.com/podcast

Blog: amyrowlinson.com/post/focus-on-magic

Chronicles of Captivity

Forty, G (1981) *Tanks Across the Desert – The War Diary of Jake Wardrop*. William Kimber.

Frankl, V E (1959, 2004) *Man's Search for Meaning*. Ebury Publishing Random House Group.

Step 1: Control

Holiday, R & Hanselman, S (2016) *The Daily Stoic: 366 meditations on wisdom, perseverance, and the art of living*. Profile Books.

Conscription: parliament.uk/about/living-heritage/transforming society/private-lives/yourcountry/overview/conscriptionww2/

Step 2: Challenge

Mass Observation: massobs.org.uk

Step 3: Capture

SDGs: un.org/sustainabledevelopment/sustainable-development-goals

CliftonStrengths: gallup.com/cliftonstrengths

Robinson, K (2006) *Do Schools Kill Creativity?* URL: ted.com/talks/ sir_ken_robinson_do_schools_kill_creativity

Step 4: Choose

Ferrer, D F (2021) 'Nietzsche's notebook of 1881: the eternal return of the same'. URL: philarchive.org/archive/FERNNO-2

Bono (2021) 'A clenched fist and an open hand: lessons learned from Desmond Tutu'. *Time.* URL: time.com/6132224/desmond-tutu-bono/

Dobrin, A (2013) 'Happiness is how you are not how you feel'. *Psychology Today* 25 January. URL: psychologytoday.com/gb/blog/am-i-right/201301/happiness-is-how-you-are-not-how-you-feel

Step 5: Create

Frankl, V E (1969, 2014) *The Will to Meaning.* Plume Penguin Group.

García, H & Miralles, F (2016) *Ikigai.* Penguin Random House.

Rani, N J & Rao, P V K (1996) 'Meditation and attention regulation'. *Journal of Indian Psychology.* URL: psycnet.apa.org/record/1997-03231-003

Sobolewski, A, Holt, E et al (2011) 'Impact of meditation on emotional processing: A visual ERP study'. *Neuroscience Research.* URL: pubmed.ncbi.nlm.nih.gov/21689695

Aurelius, M (2004) *Meditations* Translated by Maxwell Staniforth. Penguin.

Step 6: Collaborate

Brown, B (2020) *The Gifts of Imperfection.* Hazelden Publishing. NWCF: nwcf.ecb.co.uk/CFTheme

Step 7: Commit

Gast, A, Illanes, P et al (2020) 'Purpose: Shifting from why to how'. *McKinsey Quarterly* 22 April. URL: mckinsey.com/capabilities/people-and-organizational-performance/our-insights/purpose-shifting-from-why-to-how

B Corp: bcorporation.net

Step 8: Contribute

Cranston, S, Keller, S (2013) 'Increasing the 'meaning quotient' of work'. *McKinsey Quarterly* 1 January. URL: mckinsey.com/capabilities/people-and-organizational-performance/our-insights/increasing-the-meaning-quotient-of-work

Gallup (2023) 'State of the global workplace: 2023 report'. URL: gallup.com/workplace/349484/state-of-the-global-workplace.aspx

Zeno (2020). 'Unveiling the 2020 Zeno Strength of Purpose Study'. URL: zenogroup.com/insights/2020-zeno-strength-purpose

Corduneanu, R, Traynor, L et al (2022) 'Mind the Purpose Gap'. *Deloitte Insights* 20 October. URL: deloitte.com/uk/en/insights/topics/strategy/mind-the-purpose-gap

Malnight, T, Buche, I and Dhanaraj, C (2019). 'Put purpose at the core of your strategy'. Harvard Business Review. URL: hbr.org/2019/09/put-purpose-at-the-core-of-your-strategy

Claxton, G L (1998) 'Investigating human intuition: knowing without knowing why'. *Psychologist*. URL: cms.bps.org.uk/sites/default/files/2022-11/claxton98.pdf

Step 9: Change

Fotuhi, M, Mehr, S (2015) 'The science behind the powerful benefits of having a purpose'. URL: practicalneurology.com/articles/2015-sept/the-science-behind-the-powerful-benefits-of-having-a-purpose

Giannis, I & Wrosch, C et al (2023) 'Changes in purpose in life and low-grade chronic inflammation across older adulthood'. *The International Journal of Aging and Human Development*. URL: pubmed.ncbi.nlm.nih.gov/37643057

Kim, E S, Hershner, S D & Strecher, V J (2015) 'Purpose in life and incidence of sleep disturbances'. *Journal of Behavioral Medicine*. URL: pubmed.ncbi.nlm.nih.gov/25822118

Kang, Y, Cosme, D et al (2021) 'Purpose in life, loneliness, and protective health behaviors during the COVID-19 pandemic'.

Gerontologist, 13 August. URL: pubmed.ncbi.nlm.nih.gov/34125195

Friedman, E M, Hayney, M et al (2007) 'Plasma interleukin-6 and soluble IL-6 receptors are associated with psychological well-being in ageing women'. *Health Psychology* (official journal of the Division of Health Psychology, American Psychological Association). URL: pubmed.ncbi.nlm.nih.gov/17500617

Boyle, P A, Barnes, L L et al (2009) 'Purpose in life is associated with mortality among community-dwelling older persons'. *Psychosomatic Medicine.* URL: pubmed.ncbi.nlm.nih.gov/19414613

Alimujiang, A, Wiensch, A et al (2019) 'Association between life purpose and mortality among US adults older than 50 years'. *JAMA Network Open.* URL: pubmed.ncbi.nlm.nih.gov/31125099

Buettner, D (2020) *The Blue Zones of Happiness.* National Geographic Partners, LLC. URL: bluezones.com/documentary

Gale, C R, Cooper, C et al (2014) 'Psychological well-being and incident frailty in men and women: the English Longitudinal Study of Ageing'. *Psychological Medicine.* URL: pubmed.ncbi.nlm.nih.gov/23822897

Feller, S, Teucher, B et al (2013) 'Life satisfaction and risk of chronic diseases in the European prospective investigation into cancer and nutrition (EPIC) – Germany study'. *PLoS One.* URL: pubmed.ncbi.nlm.nih.gov/23977388

Lahnakoski, J M, Jääskeläinen, I P et al (2017) 'Neural mechanisms for integrating consecutive and interleaved natural events'. *Human Brain Mapping* 5 April. URL: pubmed.ncbi.nlm.nih.gov/28379608

Professional Speaking Association: thepsa.co.uk

Acknowledgements

This book is dedicated to Ruth and George. Rarely a day passes when I don't think of them – their imaginative bedtime stories, sharing laughter and giggles, late-night garden parties, feeding ducks on the pond, picking apples, listening to the magical dawn chorus. Moments I'll cherish forever.

This book didn't happen overnight; it's been an immense collaborative effort involving tough love coupled with much encouragement. First and foremost, my heartfelt gratitude goes to my mother, Catharine, who has been an absolute superstar, contributing generously countless hours of cutting, sifting and proofreading.

Thanks also to my father, Tony, for saying he'd wished he'd had this book aged 20, and for ensuring there's a lot less waffle in it!

I thank my husband, Jon, for his constant presence, love and support for more than 29 years, and for persuading me to finally press 'Send!'

I thank my children, Holly and Eddie, who have taught me many lessons in life and who continue to inspire me as they pursue their dreams and explore what's possible in life.

Thank you to my human battery charger and beautiful accountability buddy, Jo Lightfoot, who having witnessed the evolution of 'The Book' has championed me to its completion.

Love and gratitude to all the One of many™ community: to founders Dr Joanna Martin, Annie Stoker and Susie Heath who opened my eyes to possibility, meditation and dancing; thank you to mentors, Valerie Schlegel and Nathalie Baron, for skilfully guiding me to achieve OOM certification; thanks to Karen Roswell for her incredible transformative coaching; and thanks to all the women in my Lead the Change cohort, who have been on their own journeys alongside me.

Huge gratitude to the coaches and mentors who've empowered me during this book-writing journey to overcome self-imposed limitations – thank you Julie Creffield, Olga Geidane, Erin Chamberlain and Kate Trafford.

Thanks to Sue Richardson for setting up the incredible Book Buddies peer writing group. Two years later we're still going strong as Book Buddies Gone Rogue. Charlotte Jones, Chantal Cornelius, Catherine McGuire and Heather Wright, I'm so grateful for all your support. A special shout-out goes to Charlotte for sharing her invaluable insights after reading through my final draft.

Thank you also to the incredible Right Book Company team: Sue Richardson, Paul East, Andrew Chapman, Nick Redeyoff, and to Beverley Glick for her 'word witch' wisdom, reassurance and patience, particularly helping me stay focused in the final weeks.

For steering me in the right direction at the beginning of this project, thank you Dr Gilly Carr for her invaluable time and expertise and to Dr Lynda Shaw for sharing her extraordinary brain with me and for her wonderful Foreword.

Many mastermind peers have offered a word or two of encouragement, so huge thanks to: Vicky O'Farrell, Jackie Barrie, David Henson, Steve Bustin, Guy Clapperton, Peter Edge, David Hyner, Mike Pagan, Heather Townsend, Susan Heaton-Wright, Felicity Wingrove, Sharon Weinstein, Rikki Arundel, Gary Hosey, Jo Berry and Ruth Fogg.

Thank you to Jane Gunn, Tim Durkin, Helen Chorley, Vicky O'Farrell, Charlotte Jones, Kim-Adele Randall and Marcus Dimbleby for their early reader endorsements.

Thank you to Arthur Lindsay for his brilliant reading of George's parts in the audiobook version.

Although only a few of my podcast guests have been cited in the book, I want to acknowledge every one of them for their invaluable contributions in making the world a better place with their purpose-driven actions. Sharing this platform with them is a privilege, ensuring I fulfil my purpose to shine a light on just what's possible when you Focus on Why.

About the Authors

Amy Rowlinson is a life purpose coach, podcaster and speaker. Shining a light on purpose, fulfilment and curiosity to empower others to forge their own paths, Amy's chosen mission is to gift a living legacy of inspiration, insight and knowledge to create long-lasting, positive ripple effects. On her global podcast, *Focus on WHY*, Amy interviews people from all walks of life, providing uplifting and relatable conversations designed to inspire reflection with action. Amy lives in the south of England with her husband, Jon, two children, Holly and Eddie, and their springer spaniel, Rafferty.

If you're ready to create your purposeful way of life, go to amyrowlinson.com for further information.

George Fleming Kerr (1918–1996) was born in Southport, England and spent five years as a WW2 POW before dedicating the rest of his life to writing. He crafted plays for radio, television and stage in the UK and Australia, along with fiction and non-fiction books, such as *Business in Great Waters – the War History of the P. & O. 1939–1945* (1951) and *The Year of the Old Goats* (1987). Married to Ruth (1932–2022), they had one daughter, Catharine, and two grandchildren, Amy and Toby.